DO Drops
Volume 5

DO Drops

Volume 5

Daily Bible Devotional

Dr. Bo Wagner

Word of His Mouth Publishers
Mooresboro, NC

All Scripture quotations are taken from the **King James Version** of the Bible.

ISBN: 978-1-941039-15-1
Printed in the United States of America
©2021 Dr. Bo Wagner (Robert Arthur Wagner)

Word of His Mouth Publishers
Mooresboro, NC
www.wordofhismouth.com

Cover art by Chip Nuhrah

Devotion 01

Solomon finally finished the House of God, and God appeared to him once again as He had done at Gibeon.

1 Kings 9:3 *And the LORD said unto him, I have heard thy prayer and thy supplication, that thou hast made before me: I have hallowed this house, which thou hast built, to put my name there for ever; and mine eyes and mine heart shall be there perpetually.* **4** *And if thou wilt walk before me, as David thy father walked, in integrity of heart, and in uprightness, to do according to all that I have commanded thee, and wilt keep my statutes and my judgments:* **5** *Then I will establish the throne of thy kingdom upon Israel for ever, as I promised to David thy father, saying, There shall not fail thee a man upon the throne of Israel.* **6** *But if ye shall at all turn from following me, ye or your children, and will not keep my commandments and my statutes which I have set before you, but go and serve other gods, and worship them:* **7** *Then will I cut off Israel out of the land which I have given them; and this house, which I have hallowed for my name, will I cast out of my sight; and Israel shall be a proverb and a byword among all people:*

Leaving off the introductory word "And" at the beginning of verse four, what are the first words you find in verses four, five, six, and seven?

If, then, but, then. You find this scenario throughout Scripture. "IF you obey me THEN I will bless you, BUT if you disobey THEN I will blister you."

DO remember that even under the new covenant of the New Testament, this paradigm still applies in our daily living. Our eternal salvation is forever settled the moment we receive Christ, but our every day situation is largely dependent on whether we obey Him or disobey Him!

Personal Notes:

_____
_____
_____
_____
_____
_____
_____
_____
_____
_____
_____
_____
_____
_____
_____
_____
_____
_____
_____
_____
_____
_____
_____

Devotion 02

After all of Solomon's building projects were done, an amazing exchange took place between him and Hiram, the man who supplied all of the timber and labor for the twenty-year project.

1 Kings 9:10 *And it came to pass at the end of twenty years, when Solomon had built the two houses, the house of the LORD, and the king's house,* **11** *(Now Hiram the king of Tyre had furnished Solomon with cedar trees and fir trees, and with gold, according to all his desire,) that then king Solomon gave Hiram twenty cities in the land of Galilee.* **12** *And Hiram came out from Tyre to see the cities which Solomon had given him; and they pleased him not.* **13** *And he said, What cities are these which thou hast given me, my brother? And he called them the land of Cabul unto this day.*

Picture this scenario. One man works for another on a huge project for twenty solid years. At the end of that time the man he worked for gives him a payment, and the payment is, negatively, not at all what he was expecting. What do you think is the most likely response at that point? Shouting? Threats? Lawsuit?

Solomon gave Hiram twenty cities, and when Hiram took a look at them, he found them not at all to his liking. In fact, in 2 Chronicles 8:2 we learn that he actually gave them all back to Solomon! And yet, his only response was to say, "What is this, my brother?"

He refused to let a monetary disagreement ruin a friendship. That, friends, is as rare as a good idea in Congress.

DO remember that friendships are more important than "stuff" or "the stuff that buys stuff"!

Personal Notes:

_____

_____

_____

_____

_____

_____

_____

_____

_____

_____

_____

_____

_____

_____

_____

_____

_____

_____

_____

_____

_____

_____

_____

_____

_____

_____

_____

_____

_____

Devotion 03

Solomon's glory was spreading to the far corners of the globe. Thus it was that in 1 Kings 10 he received a very important visitor from afar.

1 Kings 10:1 *And when the queen of Sheba heard of the fame of Solomon concerning the name of the LORD, she came to prove him with hard questions.* **2** *And she came to Jerusalem with a very great train, with camels that bare spices, and very much gold, and precious stones: and when she was come to Solomon, she communed with him of all that was in her heart.* **3** *And Solomon told her all her questions: there was not any thing hid from the king, which he told her not.*

There is debate about the identity of this queen and exactly what country Sheba was. But there is no debate as to why she came. She had heard of Solomon's wisdom. But not just wisdom in general; she had heard of his wisdom concerning the name of the LORD! Solomon wrote books about trees and birds and animals, but none of that is why she came. She came because she heard there was a man who had great wisdom about God. And she was not going to toss him softball questions, either. Verse one says, *"she came to prove him with hard questions."*

But verse three says, *"And Solomon told her all her questions: there was not any thing hid from the king, which he told her not."* Whatever she asked about God, he knew, and he told her.

What a testimony! None of us will ever be as rich or powerful as Solomon. But all of us have the written Word of God and the indwelling Holy Spirit.

Therefore, any of us have the ability to know God just as well as Solomon did!

DO study the Word, and DO learn the God of the Word. When the world comes asking you questions, you should be ready with the answers!

Personal Notes:

_____
_____
_____
_____
_____
_____
_____
_____
_____
_____
_____
_____
_____
_____
_____
_____
_____
_____
_____
_____
_____
_____
_____
_____
_____

Devotion 04

There is an old saying, "Some things are not quite as advertised." But in Solomon's case, all of the "advertisements" were true.

1 Kings 10:4 *And when the queen of Sheba had seen all Solomon's wisdom, and the house that he had built,* **5** *And the meat of his table, and the sitting of his servants, and the attendance of his ministers, and their apparel, and his cupbearers, and his ascent by which he went up unto the house of the LORD; there was no more spirit in her.* **6** *And she said to the king, It was a true report that I heard in mine own land of thy acts and of thy wisdom.* **7** *Howbeit I believed not the words, until I came, and mine eyes had seen it: and, behold, the half was not told me: thy wisdom and prosperity exceedeth the fame which I heard.*

She came from a very long way, and she came actually expecting to be disappointed! And yet she left admitting that "*the half was not told me.*"

It is easy, especially in the days of social media, to be "not quite as advertised." I have seen photo filters that would make someone with Yoda wrinkles look like a fresh-faced teenager! And then there are all of the "spiritual giants" who definitely aren't.

Do you want to be something very special? Then DO be real! Have a great reputation for God, and make sure the reality actually matches the reputation!

Personal Notes:

Devotion 05

You could summarize verses ten through twenty-nine of 1 Kings 10 this way: gold, silver, more gold, peacocks, spices, more gold, exotic trees, more gold, gemstones, silver, more gold. How much gold did Solomon have?

1 Kings 10:21 *And all king Solomon's drinking vessels were of gold, and all the vessels of the house of the forest of Lebanon were of pure gold; none were of silver: it was nothing accounted of in the days of Solomon.*

When you have so much gold that even your Solo cups are made of it, you are loaded. Solomon was so wealthy that even silver was just no big deal anymore; it was *"nothing accounted of in the days of Solomon."*

Nothing could ever go wrong, right?

Wrong.

1 Kings 11:1 *But king Solomon loved many strange women, together with the daughter of Pharaoh, women of the Moabites, Ammonites, Edomites, Zidonians, and Hittites;* **2** *Of the nations concerning which the LORD said unto the children of Israel, Ye shall not go in to them, neither shall they come in unto you: for surely they will turn away your heart after their gods: Solomon clave unto these in love.*

Sadly, Solomon learned the hard way that there is not enough wealth on earth to buy your way out of the heartaches that come from a sordid lifestyle and wicked relationships.

Do you want to be happy and blessed? Then DO pay more attention to the balance in your "moral account" than the balance in your monetary account!

Personal Notes:

_____

_____

_____

_____

_____

_____

_____

_____

_____

_____

_____

_____

_____

_____

_____

_____

_____

_____

_____

_____

_____

_____

_____

_____

_____

_____

_____

_____

Devotion 06

One of the most horribly sad passages in the entire Bible is this one:

1 Kings 11:3 *And he had seven hundred wives, princesses, and three hundred concubines: and his wives turned away his heart. 4 For it came to pass, when Solomon was old, that his wives turned away his heart after other gods: and his heart was not perfect with the LORD his God, as was the heart of David his father. 5 For Solomon went after Ashtoreth the goddess of the Zidonians, and after Milcom the abomination of the Ammonites. 6 And Solomon did evil in the sight of the LORD, and went not fully after the LORD, as did David his father. 7 Then did Solomon build an high place for Chemosh, the abomination of Moab, in the hill that is before Jerusalem, and for Molech, the abomination of the children of Ammon. 8 And likewise did he for all his strange wives, which burnt incense and sacrificed unto their gods.*

Solomon started out higher for God and ended up lower for God than anyone else ever; his "swing" from one end to the other was far more extreme. This was the man that, when handed a blank check by God, asked for wisdom! This was the man whom the whole earth sought out to hear about God. This was the man who built the most magnificent temple to God. And this was the man who pronounced the If/Then/But/Then paradigm, reminding everyone that the blessings brought on by obedience could be lost by disobedience.

And yet when he was old, he disobeyed, horribly.

Do you realize that, while you will never have a better start than Solomon, you can easily have a better finish? Just by doing right, you will end your race better than the wisest man who ever lived.

DO right, all the way to the end!

Personal Notes:

_____

_____

_____

_____

_____

_____

_____

_____

_____

_____

_____

_____

_____

_____

_____

_____

_____

_____

_____

_____

_____

_____

_____

_____

_____

Devotion 07

Solomon did all his "marrying," and as God had warned him, it ruined him. And God was not simply going to let all of this pass by unaddressed.

1 Kings 11:9 *And the LORD was angry with Solomon, because his heart was turned from the LORD God of Israel, which had appeared unto him twice,* **10** *And had commanded him concerning this thing, that he should not go after other gods: but he kept not that which the LORD commanded.*

God's anger at Solomon was not just because he had disobeyed but also because God had appeared to him twice! In two different dreams, God actually showed up and spoke to Solomon.

There are a couple of interesting things to notice about that. One, it was such an extremely rare, unusual thing, that God expected Solomon to be in awe of it. In all of Scripture God appeared to people like this an amazingly small number of times. That ought to tell us not to be seekers after signs and wonders; the odds of God ever doing anything of the sort has always been infinitesimally small. Two, anytime God does meet with us in some way, even just through our daily Bible reading or prayer time or a good church service, it ought to do more than just "pump us up"; it ought to motivate us to holy living.

DO meet with God every way that you can and as often as you can. And DO make those meetings with Him the fertile ground out of which a holy life grows!

Personal Notes:

_____
_____
_____
_____
_____
_____
_____
_____
_____
_____
_____
_____
_____
_____
_____
_____
_____
_____
_____
_____
_____
_____
_____
_____
_____
_____

Devotion 08

Having told Solomon how angry He was over his disobedience, God then told Solomon what was going to happen because of it.

1 Kings 11:11 *Wherefore the LORD said unto Solomon, Forasmuch as this is done of thee, and thou hast not kept my covenant and my statutes, which I have commanded thee, I will surely rend the kingdom from thee, and will give it to thy servant.* **12** *Notwithstanding in thy days I will not do it for David thy father's sake: but I will rend it out of the hand of thy son.* **13** *Howbeit I will not rend away all the kingdom; but will give one tribe to thy son for David my servant's sake, and for Jerusalem's sake which I have chosen.*

When we look at the lives of David and Solomon, they both were, at times, great sinners. But in our thinking, David would be the greater sinner of the two; adultery and murder seem to trump anything Solomon ever did.

But that was not God's view. He told Solomon that he was going to take the kingdom away from him because of his sin, but that, for David's sake, he would do it after Solomon was dead, and would leave one tribe to their line. God regarded Solomon as far lesser of a godly man than David. But why? Likely because, as one old preacher observed, "Many princes have sinned with David, but few have repented with him." David repented so deeply that he actually turned his prayers of repentance into songs—Psalm 38 and 51!

DO keep yourself from sin. But when you do sin, do not simply brush it aside like Solomon, repent from the heart like David!

Personal Notes:

Devotion 09

God told Solomon he was going to take the kingdom away from his son, all but one tribe. And for the rest of the chapter, we read a list of enemies that God raised up against Solomon. Hadad the Edomite. Rezon the son of Eliadah. But the most significant of them all was Jeroboam the son of Nebat. You will hear that name a great deal from here on out in Scripture; he became the first king of the Northern tribes that split from the Southern tribes.

When Solomon realized God had appointed him to be the next king, here is how he reacted:

1 Kings 11:40 *Solomon sought therefore to kill Jeroboam...*

King realizes another will take his kingdom. King tries to kill him. Does that sound familiar? Solomon grew up hearing that exact same story; only then it was King Saul trying to kill Solomon's father, David!

How quickly people's positions change on things based on "them and theirs." DO make up your mind that right is always right and wrong is always wrong, no matter what side of the line any of "you and yours" are on!

Personal Notes:

_____
_____
_____
_____
_____
_____
_____
_____
_____
_____
_____
_____
_____
_____
_____
_____
_____
_____
_____
_____
_____
_____
_____
_____
_____

Devotion 10

Solomon, third king of Israel, died at the end of 1 Kings 11. But due to his disobedience, the glorious house of David was about to come crashing down into ignominy. Rehoboam, Solomon's son, took the throne after Solomon's death. And while Solomon ended up as far lesser of a good ruler than David, Rehoboam would be even far lesser of a good ruler than Solomon. In fact, he was such a poor leader that it took only one "business meeting" for him to cause a civil war and rip the entire kingdom apart!

1 Kings 12:12 *So Jeroboam and all the people came to Rehoboam the third day, as the king had appointed, saying, Come to me again the third day.* **13** *And the king answered the people roughly, and forsook the old men's counsel that they gave him;* **14** *And spake to them after the counsel of the young men, saying, My father made your yoke heavy, and I will add to your yoke: my father also chastised you with whips, but I will chastise you with scorpions.* **15** *Wherefore the king hearkened not unto the people; for the cause was from the LORD, that he might perform his saying, which the LORD spake by Ahijah the Shilonite unto Jeroboam the son of Nebat.* **16** *So when all Israel saw that the king hearkened not unto them, the people answered the king, saying, What portion have we in David? neither have we inheritance in the son of Jesse: to your tents, O Israel: now see to thine own house, David. So Israel departed unto their tents.*

The people simply asked for him to ease up a bit; he responded with threats, sarcasm, and haughtiness. He lost almost everything because of it.

DO learn the importance of simply being nice; it doesn't cost a thing, and it may just keep you from losing everything!

Personal Notes:

_____

_____

_____

_____

_____

_____

_____

_____

_____

_____

_____

_____

_____

_____

_____

_____

_____

_____

_____

_____

_____

_____

_____

_____

_____

_____

Devotion 11

Have you ever known a person with such a poor boss that you just had to feel sorry for them? We meet a man like that right after Rehoboam caused the civil war that split the nation. Mind you, he has just uttered the words, *"My father made your yoke heavy, and I will add to your yoke: my father also chastised you with whips, but I will chastise you with scorpions."* In other words, everyone now hates his guts and is seething angry at him. They have "seceded from his union." And it is then that Mr. "Never Will Be the Boss of the Year" does this:

1 Kings 12:18 *Then king Rehoboam sent Adoram, who was over the tribute; and all Israel stoned him with stones, that he died. Therefore king Rehoboam made speed to get him up to his chariot, to flee to Jerusalem.* **19** *So Israel rebelled against the house of David unto this day.*

He insulted and threatened everyone, split the kingdom, then sent his "tax guy" to collect the taxes from everyone that had just left him.

The tax guy got killed. Who could ever have seen that one coming?

DO realize that what you do and say will put others associated with you either in a good place or a bad place. Conduct yourself in such a way that people do not end up hating your family, workplace, church, etc. because of you!

Personal Notes:

_____
_____
_____
_____
_____
_____
_____
_____
_____
_____
_____
_____
_____
_____
_____
_____
_____
_____
_____
_____
_____
_____
_____
_____
_____
_____
_____
_____

Devotion 12

King Rehoboam seems to have done very little right or noteworthy during his reign. But here is one thing he did that neither Saul nor his father Solomon got right:

1 Kings 12:21 *And when Rehoboam was come to Jerusalem, he assembled all the house of Judah, with the tribe of Benjamin, an hundred and fourscore thousand chosen men, which were warriors, to fight against the house of Israel, to bring the kingdom again to Rehoboam the son of Solomon.* **22** *But the word of God came unto Shemaiah the man of God, saying,* **23** *Speak unto Rehoboam, the son of Solomon, king of Judah, and unto all the house of Judah and Benjamin, and to the remnant of the people, saying,* **24** *Thus saith the LORD, Ye shall not go up, nor fight against your brethren the children of Israel: return every man to his house; for this thing is from me. They hearkened therefore to the word of the LORD, and returned to depart, according to the word of the LORD.*

God told Saul he was taking the kingdom and giving it to another, and Saul responded by fighting against it and trying to kill David. God told Solomon he was taking the kingdom and giving it to another, and Solomon responded by fighting against it and trying to kill Jeroboam. But when God told Rehoboam he was taking the kingdom and giving it to Jeroboam and not to fight against him, Rehoboam obeyed. Rehoboam went down in history as one of the few kings to ever obey in a situation like that.

You may never be as famous as David or as wise as Solomon, but all of us can be as obedient as

Rehoboam! It takes no special talents or abilities to be obedient; it just takes a willing heart.

DO be obedient to the Lord, even if you really want to be disobedient!

Personal Notes:

_____

_____

_____

_____

_____

_____

_____

_____

_____

_____

_____

_____

_____

_____

_____

_____

_____

_____

_____

_____

_____

_____

_____

_____

_____

Devotion 13

Jeroboam had been given a kingdom by God. And how did he repay God for that kindness?

1 Kings 12:26 *And Jeroboam said in his heart, Now shall the kingdom return to the house of David:* **27** *If this people go up to do sacrifice in the house of the LORD at Jerusalem, then shall the heart of this people turn again unto their lord, even unto Rehoboam king of Judah, and they shall kill me, and go again to Rehoboam king of Judah.* **28** *Whereupon the king took counsel, and made two calves of gold, and said unto them, It is too much for you to go up to Jerusalem: behold thy gods, O Israel, which brought thee up out of the land of Egypt.* **29** *And he set the one in Bethel, and the other put he in Dan.* **30** *And this thing became a sin: for the people went to worship before the one, even unto Dan.*

Jeroboam made two golden calves—idols, and he set one up in the far northern extremity of his kingdom and the other in the far southern extremity of his kingdom. In so doing, he made sure that it was farther to get to Jerusalem to worship the true God than it was to get to Bethel or Dan to worship a false god. He couched all of this in terms of convenience, saying, "*It is too much for you to go up to Jerusalem...*"

Jeroboam would be very well received in modern religious circles today where devotion has been replaced with convenience. But our God, the real God, the One who made us and died for us and rose again for us, deserves our devotion. Worshiping God is never to be about convenience; it is to be about our love for the One to whom we owe everything!

DO be a Christian of devotion, not a Christian of convenience, because there actually is no such thing as a real "Christian" of convenience!

Personal Notes:

_____

_____

_____

_____

_____

_____

_____

_____

_____

_____

_____

_____

_____

_____

_____

_____

_____

_____

_____

_____

_____

_____

_____

_____

_____

_____

_____

Devotion 14

Jeroboam had set up his golden calves, but he was still not done establishing his "new way of doing church." Here was his next set of items on the agenda.

1 Kings 12:31 *And he made an house of high places, and made priests of the lowest of the people, which were not of the sons of Levi.* **32** *And Jeroboam ordained a feast in the eighth month, on the fifteenth day of the month, like unto the feast that is in Judah, and he offered upon the altar. So did he in Bethel, sacrificing unto the calves that he had made: and he placed in Bethel the priests of the high places which he had made.* **33** *So he offered upon the altar which he had made in Bethel the fifteenth day of the eighth month, even in the month which he had devised of his own heart; and ordained a feast unto the children of Israel: and he offered upon the altar, and burnt incense.*

Jeroboam appointed "men of God" who were utterly unqualified, and he also arbitrarily changed God's established ways and times of doing things. He was one of the first proponents of the modern emergent "mega church mentality." How often do you see a "superstar pastor" on tv or social media and think, "He's a preacher? Seriously?" They drink, curse, commit adultery, promote sin under the guise of tolerance, and mock anyone who stands for what the Bible actually says.

And yet, just as Jeroboam was wildly successful, they often are too. But Jeroboam did not live forever, and that means he had to stand before God one day and answer for everything. At that moment there were no adoring crowds, just the eyes of a holy God staring down in disapproval.

DO determine to do things God's way. You may end up being wildly successful, you may end up struggling along day by day, but right is always right, and the approval of God is all that really matters!

Personal Notes:

_____

_____

_____

_____

_____

_____

_____

_____

_____

_____

_____

_____

_____

_____

_____

_____

_____

_____

_____

_____

_____

_____

_____

_____

Devotion 15

1 Kings 13 is one of the most exciting, yet oddest chapters in the Bible. Jeroboam was still building his man-centered "mega-church" when suddenly a real man of God showed up like a tornado coming through a trailer park.

1 Kings 13:1 *And, behold, there came a man of God out of Judah by the word of the LORD unto Bethel: and Jeroboam stood by the altar to burn incense.* **2** *And he cried against the altar in the word of the LORD, and said, O altar, altar, thus saith the LORD; Behold, a child shall be born unto the house of David, Josiah by name; and upon thee shall he offer the priests of the high places that burn incense upon thee, and men's bones shall be burnt upon thee.* **3** *And he gave a sign the same day, saying, This is the sign which the LORD hath spoken; Behold, the altar shall be rent, and the ashes that are upon it shall be poured out.*

Earlier, Jeroboam had made priests of anybody. Now we find him taking it a step further and acting as one himself. But, when a real man of God showed up at that moment, he ripped into the idolatrous altar and the one who made it. And he also gave a very specific prophecy of a baby who would be born, grow up, destroy the altar (which would be rebuilt shortly after it was ruined in this passage) and the idolatrous priests who would be ministering at it, and even gave that future child's name, Josiah. He also gave a sign, saying that the altar would be rent, torn, and ashes poured on it.

The altar being torn happened just seconds later. But that baby being born, being named Josiah, and doing all of those very specific things? All of that happened... EXACTLY as it was foretold... 340 years later! And two bitterly rivaling nations both attest to the fact that it happened as foretold!

There is no book at all like the Bible, and there is no God at all like the God of the Bible. DO believe, every time you touch your Bible, that you are handling the very words of the living God!

Personal Notes:

_____

_____

_____

_____

_____

_____

_____

_____

_____

_____

_____

_____

_____

_____

_____

_____

_____

_____

_____

_____

_____

_____

_____

_____

_____

Devotion 16

When the man of God prophesied against Jeroboam and his altar, Jeroboam reacted violently. That did not work out so well for him.

1 Kings 13:4 *And it came to pass, when king Jeroboam heard the saying of the man of God, which had cried against the altar in Bethel, that he put forth his hand from the altar, saying, Lay hold on him. And his hand, which he put forth against him, dried up, so that he could not pull it in again to him. 5 The altar also was rent, and the ashes poured out from the altar, according to the sign which the man of God had given by the word of the LORD. 6 And the king answered and said unto the man of God, Intreat now the face of the LORD thy God, and pray for me, that my hand may be restored me again. And the man of God besought the LORD, and the king's hand was restored him again, and became as it was before.*

Jeroboam had stretched out his hand to point at the man of God as he shouted for his men to lay hold on him. But immediately his hand dried up in place, withered, lifeless, and unable to be brought back in to his body. He knew that this was both a miracle and the judgement of God against him for trying to harm the prophet of God.

And yet when he cried out to that very prophet whom just a few seconds earlier he had tried to kill, the prophet prayed for him, and he was healed. How impressive is that on the part of this prophet!

And yet it is what God still expects of us. It is natural to hold grudges, but God never called us to the natural; He called us to the supernatural. He called us to treat others as He treats us.

DO be willing to forgive; there is nothing you can ever do that makes you more like Christ than that!

Personal Notes:

_____

_____

_____

_____

_____

_____

_____

_____

_____

_____

_____

_____

_____

_____

_____

_____

_____

_____

_____

_____

_____

_____

_____

_____

_____

_____

Devotion 17

After the prophet healed Jeroboam, the king asked him to come home with him as a guest. But the prophet refused, saying, *"If thou wilt give me half thine house, I will not go in with thee, neither will I eat bread nor drink water in this place: For so was it charged me by the word of the LORD, saying, Eat no bread, nor drink water, nor turn again by the same way that thou camest."*

So, he left. And that is where the story takes a major plot twist.

1 Kings 13:11 *Now there dwelt an old prophet in Bethel; and his sons came and told him all the works that the man of God had done that day in Bethel: the words which he had spoken unto the king, them they told also to their father.* **12** *And their father said unto them, What way went he? For his sons had seen what way the man of God went, which came from Judah.* **13** *And he said unto his sons, Saddle me the ass. So they saddled him the ass: and he rode thereon,*

Where was the idolatrous altar that Jeroboam was worshiping at? Bethel. Where did this old prophet live? Bethel. And yet when God needed someone to confront the king, He called a prophet all the way from down in Judah to do it! The old prophet was right there. He could have confronted the king at any time, and yet the Bible nowhere indicates that he ever did so. As we will see in the next devotion, his following after the other prophet was calculated for destruction. But for now, just focus in on the fact that God had to send someone from many miles away to do what he could have done right there where he lived.

When God looks around at your family, job, school, etc. make sure that He sees in you someone that He can count on to stand up and speak truth! DO make sure He does not have to look to someone in another county, state, or country to come and do what you could and should be doing yourself!

Personal Notes:

_____

_____

_____

_____

_____

_____

_____

_____

_____

_____

_____

_____

_____

_____

_____

_____

_____

_____

_____

_____

_____

_____

_____

_____

_____

Devotion 18

The old "do-nothing" prophet went after and caught up with the young prophet from Judah. He asked him to come home with him for a while, and the young prophet repeated the exact same words to him he had said to Jeroboam, letting him know that God told him not to go back there. Sadly, though that should be the end of the story, it isn't.

1 Kings 13:18 *He said unto him, I am a prophet also as thou art; and an angel spake unto me by the word of the LORD, saying, Bring him back with thee into thine house, that he may eat bread and drink water. But he lied unto him.*

He lied. Intentionally. Knowing what would happen. And the young prophet fell for it:

1 Kings 13:20 *And it came to pass, as they sat at the table, that the word of the LORD came unto the prophet that brought him back:* **21** *And he cried unto the man of God that came from Judah, saying, Thus saith the LORD, Forasmuch as thou hast disobeyed the mouth of the LORD, and hast not kept the commandment which the LORD thy God commanded thee,* **22** *But camest back, and hast eaten bread and drunk water in the place, of the which the LORD did say to thee, Eat no bread, and drink no water; thy carcase shall not come unto the sepulchre of thy fathers.* **23** *And it came to pass, after he had eaten bread, and after he had drunk, that he saddled for him the ass, to wit, for the prophet whom he had brought back.* **24** *And when he was gone, a lion met him by the way, and slew him: and his carcase was cast in the way, and the ass stood by it, the lion also stood by the carcase.*

The young prophet lost his life for disobeying God. But why did he disobey God? Simply because he took someone's word without considering that someone's character. If that old prophet lived in Bethel, he should have confronted Jeroboam, but never did! This was a man who could not be trusted.

DO be polite and pleasant, yet always pay attention and have your guard up as well. This guy died because another guy lied, and he was not cautious enough to pay attention!

Personal Notes:

_____

_____

_____

_____

_____

_____

_____

_____

_____

_____

_____

_____

_____

_____

_____

_____

_____

_____

_____

_____

Devotion 19

The old, do-nothing prophet had subtly brought about the death of the real man of God sent from Judah. What happened next gives me one of those forehead in the palm kind of reactions:

1 Kings 13:27 *And he spake to his sons, saying, Saddle me the ass. And they saddled him.* **28** *And he went and found his carcase cast in the way, and the ass and the lion standing by the carcase: the lion had not eaten the carcase, nor torn the ass.* **29** *And the prophet took up the carcase of the man of God, and laid it upon the ass, and brought it back: and the old prophet came to the city, to mourn and to bury him.* **30** *And he laid his carcase in his own grave; and they mourned over him, saying, Alas, my brother!* **31** *And it came to pass, after he had buried him, that he spake to his sons, saying, When I am dead, then bury me in the sepulchre wherein the man of God is buried; lay my bones beside his bones:*

How sweet! (Sarcasm). This precious old prophet was so sad over the death of the young prophet that he mourned over his loss, carried him home, buried him in his own grave, and asked to be buried beside him when he died.

All of which would be so very touching, if he himself had not been the cause of the man's death!

Weeping over a loss is nowhere near as "precious" as not being the cause of that loss to begin with.

Whether it be a marriage, a church family, a friendship, a family tie, DO give much more thought to not causing harm to begin with than you do to putting on a good performance of mourning after you do!

Personal Notes:

_____

_____

_____

_____

_____

_____

_____

_____

_____

_____

_____

_____

_____

_____

_____

_____

_____

_____

_____

_____

_____

_____

_____

_____

_____

_____

_____

_____

_____

Devotion 20

King Jeroboam had experienced quite a shock. He had been confronted by a true man of God. He had been stricken with a withered hand when he reached out against him. He had been miraculously healed when the prophet prayed for him. His altar had been supernaturally ruined. One would think that all of that would surely be enough to convince him to amend his ways. And one would be wrong in so thinking.

1 Kings 13:33 *After this thing Jeroboam returned not from his evil way, but made again of the lowest of the people priests of the high places: whosoever would, he consecrated him, and he became one of the priests of the high places.* **34** *And this thing became sin unto the house of Jeroboam, even to cut it off, and to destroy it from off the face of the earth.*

The particular condemnation leveled against Jeroboam in this passage is a shocking one when compared to the "standard, accepted practice of our day." Jeroboam made priests, clergy, "men of God," out of *"whosoever would."* Simply put, no matter who wanted to be in the ministry, Jeroboam was in favor of it! All of the qualifications God laid out for the ministry were utterly ignored.

Welcome to Israel, circa 975 B.C., and America, circa late twentieth and early twenty-first century. "He drinks, curses, committed adultery, and has been married multiple times? Who cares; look at the crowd he draws! Look at his million plus online followers! Let's retweet and share his every word and send money to his ministry!"

If they are looking for a "lit" name for such a church, I would recommend "Jeroboam Church."

DO expect men of God to meet the qualifications laid out by Scripture, and DO refuse to follow those who don't!

Personal Notes:

_____

_____

_____

_____

_____

_____

_____

_____

_____

_____

_____

_____

_____

_____

_____

_____

_____

_____

_____

_____

_____

_____

_____

_____

_____

_____

_____

Devotion 21

"Jeroboam Church" rocked on for a while with their unqualified clergy, but eventually, the good times ran into a rock wall of problem.

1 Kings 14:1 *At that time Abijah the son of Jeroboam fell sick.* **2** *And Jeroboam said to his wife, Arise, I pray thee, and disguise thyself, that thou be not known to be the wife of Jeroboam; and get thee to Shiloh: behold, there is Ahijah the prophet, which told me that I should be king over this people.* **3** *And take with thee ten loaves, and cracknels, and a cruse of honey, and go to him: he shall tell thee what shall become of the child.*

King Jeroboam himself started the unqualified clergy nonsense. But when his own son fell grievously ill and he found himself in need of a man of God, notice that he did not even bother to contact a single one of the hirelings he had put in place! He bypassed Bethel and Dan, where his golden calf worship was happening and sent his wife to Shiloh to visit Ahijah, an actual man of God.

It is amazing how often that happens. Jeroboam Church and the cursing, drinking, carousing, rocking clergy are great for the concerts that masquerade as worship. But when a marriage ends up in tatters, or a child gets into trouble, or a loved one dies, people instinctively seek out the real man of God from wherever they used to be, because they know they can find the help they need there.

Which ought to tell them that they never should have forsaken Ahijah for Jeroboam Church to begin with.

If you have a real church and a real man of God, never leave for a Jeroboam Church. DO be faithful to the ones who will always be there in your hour of greatest need!

Personal Notes:

_____

_____

_____

_____

_____

_____

_____

_____

_____

_____

_____

_____

_____

_____

_____

_____

_____

_____

_____

_____

_____

_____

_____

Devotion 22

Perhaps the oddest thing about Jeroboam sending his wife to Ahijah the prophet was his instruction that she disguise herself. He was sending her to Ahijah to get a word from God on whether their son would live or die.

Do you see the irony? If Ahijah was able to know that, how did they think that he would somehow not know who she was?

Turns out he did know. Even before she arrived.

1 Kings 14:5 *And the LORD said unto Ahijah, Behold, the wife of Jeroboam cometh to ask a thing of thee for her son; for he is sick: thus and thus shalt thou say unto her: for it shall be, when she cometh in, that she shall feign herself to be another woman.* **6** *And it was so, when Ahijah heard the sound of her feet, as she came in at the door, that he said, Come in, thou wife of Jeroboam; why feignest thou thyself to be another? for I am sent to thee with heavy tidings.*

Heavy tidings indeed. He gave her the last message she wanted to hear—her son was going to die because of her husband's wickedness. In fact, he would die as soon as her feet entered the city to get back to him; she would never hold his living body again.

But the most shocking part of it all, in a good way, is found in verse thirteen.

1 Kings 14:13 *And all Israel shall mourn for him, and bury him: for he only of Jeroboam shall come to the grave, because in him there is found some good thing toward the LORD God of Israel in the house of Jeroboam.*

It was, at least in part, the mercy of God that the boy died. There was still something in his heart that yearned for the God of Israel, and God would not allow him to get old enough to lose that and become a lost reprobate like his father.

I wonder how often that very same type of thing happens? How often does God in mercy end a life early before a person comes to ruin?

DO understand that even in the worst of circumstances, God is always looking ahead in mercy, and those horrible circumstances themselves may be the vessel delivering that mercy!

Personal Notes:

_____

_____

_____

_____

_____

_____

_____

_____

_____

_____

_____

_____

_____

_____

_____

_____

_____

_____

Devotion 23

For a good while the focus has been on Jeroboam and the Northern Kingdom, his golden calves, and his unqualified clergy. He started a wicked ball rolling that did not stop for several hundred years.

But finally, our attention is turned back south to Judah and Solomon's son, King Rehoboam.

1 Kings 14:21 *And Rehoboam the son of Solomon reigned in Judah. Rehoboam was forty and one years old when he began to reign, and he reigned seventeen years in Jerusalem, the city which the LORD did choose out of all the tribes of Israel, to put his name there. And his mother's name was Naamah an Ammonitess.* **22** *And Judah did evil in the sight of the LORD, and they provoked him to jealousy with their sins which they had committed, above all that their fathers had done.* **23** *For they also built them high places, and images, and groves, on every high hill, and under every green tree.* **24** *And there were also sodomites in the land: and they did according to all the abominations of the nations which the LORD cast out before the children of Israel.*

As wicked as Jeroboam and the northern kingdom were, Rehoboam and the southern kingdom matched them stride for stride! This is all the more shocking when we realize that Rehoboam, the son of Solomon, had a powerful written guide to go by to keep him and his kingdom from evil.

His father wrote the book of Proverbs for him.

Talk about ignoring good counsel!

Throughout your life you will be given a great deal of very good counsel. As long as it hits you and rolls right off it will be of none effect. Truth cannot be worn as a decoration; it must be internalized as a guide.

DO internalize the truth of Scripture and any truth from others that goes along with the truth of Scripture!

Personal Notes:

_____

_____

_____

_____

_____

_____

_____

_____

_____

_____

_____

_____

_____

_____

_____

_____

_____

_____

_____

_____

_____

_____

_____

_____

_____

_____

Devotion 24

Due to Rehoboam's wickedness, God sent an enemy against Judah, and that enemy took some very precious things:

1 Kings 14:25 *And it came to pass in the fifth year of king Rehoboam, that Shishak king of Egypt came up against Jerusalem:* **26** *And he took away the treasures of the house of the LORD, and the treasures of the king's house; he even took away all: and he took away all the shields of gold which Solomon had made.*

Specifically mentioned in the treasures that Shishak took from Judah and Rehoboam was the shields of gold that King Solomon had made back in 1 Kings 10:17. There were three hundred of them, and each shield contained three pounds of gold! Gold is measured in troy ounces, so at today's price of around $1,866 per ounce those shields would be worth more than twenty million dollars in today's money!

Rehoboam, due to his sin, lost them. The next logical step would be to repent, get right with God, and go get them back. But Rehoboam took a different approach.

1 Kings 14:27 *And king Rehoboam made in their stead brasen shields, and committed them unto the hands of the chief of the guard, which kept the door of the king's house.*

To the untrained eye, brass and gold look very much alike. Rehoboam made counterfeits to cover up for losing the real thing. How very much he sounds like people today.

Never settle for spiritual counterfeits. If your sin ever costs you something, and it will, DO repent, DO get right with God, and as much as is still possible, DO get back to where you were and recover what you lost! The real thing is much better than the "virtual spirituality and blessings" people brag about online to cover up the fact that the golden shields have been gone for a very long time!

Personal Notes:

_____

_____

_____

_____

_____

_____

_____

_____

_____

_____

_____

_____

_____

_____

_____

_____

_____

_____

_____

_____

_____

_____

_____

_____

_____

Devotion 25

After the death of King Rehoboam of Judah, Abijam, his son, took the throne. And while his father and grandfather and great grandfather had reigned for relatively long periods of time, Abijam lasted only three years. And they were not a good three years:

1 Kings 15:3 *And he walked in all the sins of his father, which he had done before him: and his heart was not perfect with the LORD his God, as the heart of David his father.*

His sinful father was Rehoboam. The righteous influence in his family history had been his "father," David, who was actually his great grandfather. So, when God wanted to point to a bad example for Abijam, He pointed to his father, Rehoboam, and when He wanted to point to a good example for Abijam, He pointed to his great grandfather, David.

Solomon was left out of the picture. Solomon, who wrote the book of Proverbs for him, was left out of the picture. You see, Solomon wrote one way and then later lived another way entirely. So, the totality of his influence on his son was mixed between good and bad, and God thus refused to even mention him in this place.

DO know that children watch both what you say and what you do, and they watch that way forever. You will not get a pass on hypocrisy, nor should you, so DO instruct right and make sure your own life matches those instructions!

Personal Notes:

Devotion 26

After the death of Abijam, Asa took the throne of Judah. He did so at a time when things had been going steadily downhill in the nation for many years. His great grandfather, Solomon, strayed from God in his later years and went after women and idols. Then his grandfather, Rehoboam, took the nation a much greater distance down the path of idolatry. Then his father, Abijam, kept the nation on that same course.

In other words, by the time he took the throne, "times had changed," and society was okay with the wickedness of the day. But God was not okay with it and neither was the new king.

1 Kings 15:11 *And Asa did that which was right in the eyes of the LORD, as did David his father.* **12** *And he took away the sodomites out of the land, and removed all the idols that his fathers had made.* **13** *And also Maachah his mother, even her he removed from being queen, because she had made an idol in a grove; and Asa destroyed her idol, and burnt it by the brook Kidron.*

This man cleaned house, not just in the nation but in his own family! That takes courage, especially when one will be viewed as being "old fashioned and out of step with the times."

DO determine that your view of right and wrong will never be determined by what is now acceptable to society. Times change, but God's view of sin never changes with them!

Personal Notes:

_____
_____
_____
_____
_____
_____
_____
_____
_____
_____
_____
_____
_____
_____
_____
_____
_____
_____
_____
_____
_____
_____
_____
_____
_____
_____

Devotion 27

Back up north, in Israel, wicked Jeroboam died, and his son, Nadab, took the throne. He only lasted for two years before he was murdered by a man named Baasha. But Baasha did not just kill him, he killed many, many more.

1 Kings 15:28 *Even in the third year of Asa king of Judah did Baasha slay him* [Nadab], *and reigned in his stead.* **29** *And it came to pass, when he reigned, that he smote all the house of Jeroboam; he left not to Jeroboam any that breathed, until he had destroyed him, according unto the saying of the LORD, which he spake by his servant Ahijah the Shilonite:* **30** *Because of the sins of Jeroboam which he sinned, and which he made Israel sin, by his provocation wherewith he provoked the LORD God of Israel to anger.*

Baasha totally wiped out the house of Jeroboam. This is what God told Jeroboam was going to happen because of the sin that Jeroboam took the entire nation into. Jeroboam sent countless numbers to hell over hundreds of years because of the golden calves which he made, which could never seem to be totally eradicated. Little wonder that God reacted against his household in such anger. It is one thing to reject God yourself; it is quite another to enthusiastically convince others to do so.

There are many people like him in our day. When you see and hear them and get so very angry at what they do, DO remember that God always settles accounts, and this kind of account He always settles harshly!

Personal Notes:

_____
_____
_____
_____
_____
_____
_____
_____
_____
_____
_____
_____
_____
_____
_____
_____
_____
_____
_____
_____
_____
_____
_____
_____
_____
_____
_____
_____

Devotion 28

You will find that throughout the history of the Northern Kingdom, Israel, there was not a single godly king at all. All of them were wicked to the core. God used Baasha to judge and destroy Nadab and all the line of Jeroboam, then Baasha turned right around and led in the same wicked way that they had.

1 Kings 16:1 *Then the word of the LORD came to Jehu the son of Hanani against Baasha, saying,* **2** *Forasmuch as I exalted thee out of the dust, and made thee prince over my people Israel; and thou hast walked in the way of Jeroboam, and hast made my people Israel to sin, to provoke me to anger with their sins;* **3** *Behold, I will take away the posterity of Baasha, and the posterity of his house; and will make thy house like the house of Jeroboam the son of Nebat.* **4** *Him that dieth of Baasha in the city shall the dogs eat; and him that dieth of his in the fields shall the fowls of the air eat.* **5** *Now the rest of the acts of Baasha, and what he did, and his might, are they not written in the book of the chronicles of the kings of Israel?*

According to verse five, Baasha was a mighty man. But that power did not keep him and his entire family from dying and dying in such an ignominious way that they did not even get to be buried. No human "might" is enough to stay the hand of God's judgement on those who defy Him.

The good news on the flip side of that coin is that no human weakness is enough to keep God's hand of blessing off of those who obey.

DO obey God; He would much rather bless you than blister you!

Personal Notes:

_____

_____

_____

_____

_____

_____

_____

_____

_____

_____

_____

_____

_____

_____

_____

_____

_____

_____

_____

_____

_____

_____

_____

_____

_____

_____

Devotion 29

After king Baasha of Israel died, his son, Elah, took the throne. It was a short reign with an inglorious ending:

1 Kings 16:8 *In the twenty and sixth year of Asa king of Judah began Elah the son of Baasha to reign over Israel in Tirzah, two years. 9 And his servant Zimri, captain of half his chariots, conspired against him, as he was in Tirzah, drinking himself drunk in the house of Arza steward of his house in Tirzah. 10 And Zimri went in and smote him, and killed him, in the twenty and seventh year of Asa king of Judah, and reigned in his stead.*

I passed a billboard by the interstate recently. It had a picture of a man holding a bottle, and the words "He's a drunk." But the word "drunk" had been exed out in red, and below that was the phrase "words hurt." The message of the sign was clear—don't call people drunks; we must avoid hurting anyone's feelings.

I am quite sure King Elah would have been "hurt" over the use of the word drunk as well. But what really hurt was getting murdered and being too drunk to stop it from happening.

DO stay away from alcoholic beverages, period. No one ever got drunk without putting the bottle to their lips for the first time. And if you are a drunk, DO worry more about your drunkenness than you do your "hurt feelings" over someone loving you enough to confront you about it!

Personal Notes:

_____

_____

_____

_____

_____

_____

_____

_____

_____

_____

_____

_____

_____

_____

_____

_____

_____

_____

_____

_____

_____

_____

_____

_____

_____

_____

_____

_____

_____

Devotion 30

Zimri killed Elah and took the throne of Israel. But he was about to set the record for "least time in office before getting oneself killed."

1 Kings 16:15 *In the twenty and seventh year of Asa king of Judah did Zimri reign seven days in Tirzah. And the people were encamped against Gibbethon, which belonged to the Philistines.* **16** *And the people that were encamped heard say, Zimri hath conspired, and hath also slain the king: wherefore all Israel made Omri, the captain of the host, king over Israel that day in the camp.* **17** *And Omri went up from Gibbethon, and all Israel with him, and they besieged Tirzah.* **18** *And it came to pass, when Zimri saw that the city was taken, that he went into the palace of the king's house, and burnt the king's house over him with fire, and died,* **19** *For his sins which he sinned in doing evil in the sight of the LORD, in walking in the way of Jeroboam, and in his sin which he did, to make Israel to sin.*

Seven days. Just seven days on the throne, and he realized he was about to lose that throne. Rather than face the music, he committed suicide by burning the palace down with himself inside. This was one last vindictive, spiteful act from a wicked man. If he was going to die, he determined to burn the palace to the ground as he did and leave nothing but a pile of rubble for the next king.

Vindictiveness is always like that, and no one ever benefits from it.

DO determine to be the least vindictive person in the world. Vindictive people leave rubble; selfless people leave a legacy.

Personal Notes:

Devotion 31

As if a civil war that split one nation into two was not bad enough, for a time there was actually a civil war within one side of the civil war.

1 Kings 16:21 *Then were the people of Israel divided into two parts: half of the people followed Tibni the son of Ginath, to make him king; and half followed Omri.* **22** *But the people that followed Omri prevailed against the people that followed Tibni the son of Ginath: so Tibni died, and Omri reigned.*

It is almost amusing the casual way we read "so Tibni died, and Omri reigned." What those few words mean is that both of them were vying for the throne, one of them came out on top, so the other one was put to death. It is as if there was never any middle ground; whoever wins, lives; whoever loses, dies.

As bad as that is in a nation, that pattern often somewhat reoccurs in homes in our own day. An argument over some issue ensues, and both sides prepare to do battle to the death over it. It causes the death of a marriage, the death of love, the death of a family, the death of a future. No one seems to realize that not every contest has to have a loser.

DO make up your mind that in your home, every conflict will be resolved in such a way that everyone comes out of it better than they went into it!

Personal Notes:

_____
_____
_____
_____
_____
_____
_____
_____
_____
_____
_____
_____
_____
_____
_____
_____
_____
_____
_____
_____
_____
_____
_____
_____
_____
_____
_____

Devotion 32

After dispatching Tibni, Omri took the throne in the Northern Kingdom, Israel. His reign was an evil one, 1 Kings 16:25 says that he "*did worse than all that were before him.*" Little wonder, then, that he would end up having a son who became legendary all the way into our day thousands of years later for his own wickedness:

1 Kings 16:29 *And in the thirty and eighth year of Asa king of Judah began Ahab the son of Omri to reign over Israel: and Ahab the son of Omri reigned over Israel in Samaria twenty and two years.* **30** *And Ahab the son of Omri did evil in the sight of the LORD above all that were before him.* **31** *And it came to pass, as if it had been a light thing for him to walk in the sins of Jeroboam the son of Nebat, that he took to wife Jezebel the daughter of Ethbaal king of the Zidonians, and went and served Baal, and worshipped him.* **32** *And he reared up an altar for Baal in the house of Baal, which he had built in Samaria.* **33** *And Ahab made a grove; and Ahab did more to provoke the LORD God of Israel to anger than all the kings of Israel that were before him.*

Ahab married the most wicked woman on the face of the planet, Jezebel, and he also made an altar for Baal right there in Samaria. Ahab became the measuring stick for wickedness for every future king, and no one ever fully measured up to him.

DO become a measuring stick in your home, church, business, school, everywhere. But become a measuring stick for righteousness, not wickedness! Let future generations use you as a pattern of what it means to be a real child of God.

Personal Notes:

Devotion 33

For king after king, year after year, generation after generation, it had been all wickedness all the time among the kings of Israel, and because of them, in the nation itself. It seemed that nothing could ever change that dynamic. But then something did...

1 Kings 17:1 *And Elijah the Tishbite, who was of the inhabitants of Gilead, said unto Ahab, As the LORD God of Israel liveth, before whom I stand, there shall not be dew nor rain these years, but according to my word.*

From seemingly out of nowhere, a man named Elijah burst onto the scene. All we know about him prior to this is that he was from the city of Tishbeh in the land of Gilead. But this one man, all by himself, confronted powerful, wicked King Ahab and pronounced judgment on all the land because of his wickedness. For three and a half years not a drop of rain fell and not a bit of dew formed. Elijah's impact was so great that he goes on to be mentioned by name ninety-nine times in the Bible, including in all four gospels, Romans, and James. John the Baptist came *"in the spirit and power of Elias* [Elijah]," Jesus was assumed to be a resurrected Elijah, Elijah met with Jesus and Moses on the Mount of Transfiguration, and it is highly likely that he is one of the two God-empowered witnesses during the Tribulation Period.

Not bad for a nobody from nowhere.

DO know that God can use you mightily and wants to do so, even if you are a nobody from nowhere. In fact, that seems to be His favorite kind of person to use, since that way He easily gets all of the glory!

Personal Notes:

_____
_____
_____
_____
_____
_____
_____
_____
_____
_____
_____
_____
_____
_____
_____
_____
_____
_____
_____
_____
_____
_____
_____
_____
_____
_____
_____
_____

Devotion 34

Once Elijah burst onto the scene and confronted Ahab, his life was immediately at risk. So God put him into "The Witness Protection Program."

1 Kings 17:2 *And the word of the LORD came unto him, saying, 3 Get thee hence, and turn thee eastward, and hide thyself by the brook Cherith, that is before Jordan. 4 And it shall be, that thou shalt drink of the brook; and I have commanded the ravens to feed thee there. 5 So he went and did according unto the word of the LORD: for he went and dwelt by the brook Cherith, that is before Jordan. 6 And the ravens brought him bread and flesh in the morning, and bread and flesh in the evening; and he drank of the brook.*

A man drinking from a brook is not so remarkable. But a man being fed by ravens, twice a day every day, is unthinkable. The pertinent facts about ravens are as follows: first, ravens care only about themselves, second, ravens care only about themselves, and third, ravens care only about themselves.

And yet our God is so sovereign that He is able to command ravens to do pick-up and delivery twice a day for His hungry prophet. Thousands of years before "Grubhub" and "DoorDash" there was "Foodflight."

DO spend every day in the calm realization that when you are in God's will, His supplies for the day are always "winging their way to your location"!

Personal Notes:

_____
_____
_____
_____
_____
_____
_____
_____
_____
_____
_____
_____
_____
_____
_____
_____
_____
_____
_____
_____
_____
_____
_____
_____
_____
_____
_____

Devotion 35

Elijah was God's man, but he was also, like every believer, God's pupil. And he was about to learn another lesson.

1 Kings 17:7 *And it came to pass after a while, that the brook dried up, because there had been no rain in the land.* **8** *And the word of the LORD came unto him, saying,* **9** *Arise, get thee to Zarephath, which belongeth to Zidon, and dwell there: behold, I have commanded a widow woman there to sustain thee.*

Elijah, no doubt, enjoyed his quiet, peaceful time by the babbling brook and the twice-a-day food delivery service from Foodflight. But after a while, in the center of God's will, having done nothing at all wrong, the brook dried up.

Have you ever been there? It isn't easy, is it!

But the same God that sent Elijah to that brook had already made provisions for the next step of the journey. He was to go to Zarephath; God had commanded a widow woman there to take care of him.

You will often find yourself in those "brook-drying-up" situations. You examine your life, see that you are not in sin, you are in God's will, and you wonder, therefore, why God would allow the brook to dry up.

But if the brook had never dried up, Elijah would have been there forever. And God had greater things planned for him. So, when your brook dries up, DO remember that God is using its drying up just as surely as He used its flowing waters, and that He is using it to get you to the next great step along your journey!

Personal Notes:

_____

_____

_____

_____

_____

_____

_____

_____

_____

_____

_____

_____

_____

_____

_____

_____

_____

_____

_____

_____

_____

_____

_____

_____

_____

_____

Devotion 36

When Elijah got to Zarephath, he found a pitiful site waiting for him.

1 Kings 17:10 *So he arose and went to Zarephath. And when he came to the gate of the city, behold, the widow woman was there gathering of sticks: and he called to her, and said, Fetch me, I pray thee, a little water in a vessel, that I may drink.* **11** *And as she was going to fetch it, he called to her, and said, Bring me, I pray thee, a morsel of bread in thine hand.* **12** *And she said, As the LORD thy God liveth, I have not a cake, but an handful of meal in a barrel, and a little oil in a cruse: and, behold, I am gathering two sticks, that I may go in and dress it for me and my son, that we may eat it, and die.*

Hard times had fallen on Zarephath, just like everywhere else. Suddenly, a man showed up and asked this lady for food and water. The water she could provide a little of, but the food she said she could not. She had just enough for one last meal for herself and her son. Her plan, in her own words, was for her and her son to "eat that last meal then die."

That is a horrible plan, but at that moment, it was all she had. But then Elijah gave her another plan:

1 Kings 17:13 *And Elijah said unto her, Fear not; go and do as thou hast said: but make me thereof a little cake first, and bring it unto me, and after make for thee and for thy son.* **14** *For thus saith the LORD God of Israel, The barrel of meal shall not waste, neither shall the cruse of oil fail, until the day that the LORD sendeth rain upon the earth.* **15** *And she went and did according to the saying of Elijah: and she, and he, and her house, did eat many days.*

This plan would require her to step out on faith, but perhaps not as great of a step of faith as you think. If he was wrong, she would simply die one day sooner than expected! So, Elijah's plan truly was the more reasonable of the two because it actually gave her and her son a chance to live.

DO remember that, while God expects us to step out on faith and believe Him, when it gets right down to it, His plan is so very reasonable that it only makes sense for us to do so!

Personal Notes:

_____
_____
_____
_____
_____
_____
_____
_____
_____
_____
_____
_____
_____
_____
_____
_____
_____
_____
_____
_____

Devotion 37

Elijah had arrived in Zarephath and met the widow woman whom God had prepared to sustain him while he was there. Upon asking for food, she had informed him that she only had enough for one more meal for herself and her son, and they were going to eat it and then die. Elijah told her to step out on faith; she was to fix him a meal first and then trust this promise:

1 Kings 17:14 *For thus saith the LORD God of Israel, The barrel of meal shall not waste, neither shall the cruse of oil fail, until the day that the LORD sendeth rain upon the earth.*

That was quite the step of faith he was asking for. But she responded well, and God honored His promise:

1 Kings 17:15 *And she went and did according to the saying of Elijah: and she, and he, and her house, did eat many days.* **16** *And the barrel of meal wasted not, neither did the cruse of oil fail, according to the word of the LORD, which he spake by Elijah.*

Many days. The barrel that only had enough for one more day lasted many days, as did the cruse of oil. The same God that performed an overwhelmingly huge and obvious miracle in withholding rain and dew from all the land for more than three years, also handled a "one-house miracle," something utterly personal.

DO remember that God is just as pleased to do a "one-house miracle" for you as He is to perform a nationwide miracle for all. God knows and cares about individuals, including you!

78

Personal Notes:

Devotion 38

We often say, "God has a reason for everything He does." And while that statement is true, it is also usually woefully lacking. It is normally more accurate to say, "God has a great many reasons for everything He does." For instance, God sent Elijah to Zarephath, to a widow's house. Why? The obvious reason is to feed Elijah and keep him alive.

But there was another reason as well.

1 Kings 17:17 *And it came to pass after these things, that the son of the woman, the mistress of the house, fell sick; and his sickness was so sore, that there was no breath left in him.* **18** *And she said unto Elijah, What have I to do with thee, O thou man of God? art thou come unto me to call my sin to remembrance, and to slay my son?*

Somewhere along the line, this woman had a sin issue. It was so troubling her that, when her son died, she assumed her sin was the cause of it. Not one word about sin had yet been spoken in the text, but having the prophet there was so convicting to her, that she began to feel the weight of guilt over it.

The rest of the story, as Paul Harvey would say, is that Elijah raised the boy back to life, and the woman began to express faith in the word of the LORD in verse twenty-four. So, God did not just send Elijah to the woman so the woman could help him with his physical needs, He also sent him there so Elijah could help the woman with her spiritual needs.

Every day, and in every circumstance of your day, DO know that God is likely to alter your circumstances and schedules just to bring you into contact with those who need to know God. So DO be ready to tell them about Him!

Personal Notes:

_____

_____

_____

_____

_____

_____

_____

_____

_____

_____

_____

_____

_____

_____

_____

_____

_____

_____

_____

_____

_____

_____

_____

_____

_____

_____

Devotion 39

After more than three years of absolute drought and famine, God spoke to Elijah. And the words He spoke to him were frightening words.

1 Kings 18:1 *And it came to pass after many days, that the word of the LORD came to Elijah in the third year, saying, Go, shew thyself unto Ahab; and I will send rain upon the earth.*

To say that Ahab hated Elijah would be an understatement. To say that Ahab's wife, Jezebel, hated Elijah, would be an understatement of Noahic flood proportions. Both of them would be willing to kill him at the drop of a hat, and, as king, Ahab had the earthly power to do it. And yet here was God saying to Elijah, "*Go show yourself to Ahab; and I will send rain upon the earth.*"

Elijah had been well fed and well taken care of throughout the drought. Why should he risk his neck like that? Well, other than "because God said so," how about the fact that people were dying all around him.

And so he went.

1 Kings 18:2 *And Elijah went to shew himself unto Ahab. And there was a sore famine in Samaria.*

This was the first step in breaking the drought. Elijah was commissioned to go, and he did. How often, I wonder, do we experience a spiritual drought because God's people only think about themselves and their welfare and give no thought to those drying up and dying without God?

DO give thought to others; don't just go to heaven yourself. DO whatever is necessary to bring others with you!

Personal Notes:

_____
_____
_____
_____
_____
_____
_____
_____
_____
_____
_____
_____
_____
_____
_____
_____
_____
_____
_____
_____
_____
_____
_____
_____
_____
_____
_____
_____

Devotion 40

For the last two chapters of Scripture, Elijah has stood alone, a towering figure of greatness for God. But as we get into the next couple of verses, another great man for God is brought to our attention, a very different kind of man, showing greatness in his own unique way.

1 Kings 18:3 A*nd Ahab called Obadiah, which was the governor of his house. (Now Obadiah feared the LORD greatly:* **4** *For it was so, when Jezebel cut off the prophets of the LORD, that Obadiah took an hundred prophets, and hid them by fifty in a cave, and fed them with bread and water.)* **5** *And Ahab said unto Obadiah, Go into the land, unto all fountains of water, and unto all brooks: peradventure we may find grass to save the horses and mules alive, that we lose not all the beasts.*

This man Obadiah, a different Obadiah than the prophet for whom the book of Obadiah is named, was the governor of Ahab's house... and also a devout believer in Jehovah God. He saved the lives of one hundred prophets, hid them, and fed them all during the drought. This was a very risky thing for Obadiah; had he been caught, Jezebel would doubtless have tortured and/or killed him.

Obadiah was no Elijah. Elijah was an out in the open, in your face, showdown at high noon prophet of God. That is what God needed him to be and called him to be. But Obadiah, while very different from Elijah, was no less important, especially to one hundred men whose lives he saved!

You are not like anyone else. Don't ever try to be like anyone else. God made you and equipped you just like He wanted to, and there is not another you. So, DO be YOU for God!

Personal Notes:

_____
_____
_____
_____
_____
_____
_____
_____
_____
_____
_____
_____
_____
_____
_____
_____
_____
_____
_____
_____
_____
_____
_____
_____
_____
_____
_____
_____
_____

Devotion 41

Ahab and Obadiah had divided the land and were searching through it trying to find some grass still living to save some of the beasts alive. The fact that the king himself was having to do half of the search shows just how desperate things had gotten!

But as Obadiah was searching his half, he came across a very familiar figure.

1 Kings 18:7 *And as Obadiah was in the way, behold, Elijah met him: and he knew him, and fell on his face, and said, Art thou that my lord Elijah?* **8** *And he answered him, I am: go, tell thy lord, Behold, Elijah is here.* **9** *And he said, What have I sinned, that thou wouldest deliver thy servant into the hand of Ahab, to slay me?* **10** *As the LORD thy God liveth, there is no nation or kingdom, whither my lord hath not sent to seek thee: and when they said, He is not there; he took an oath of the kingdom and nation, that they found thee not.*

The words of Obadiah give us insight into something that was going on during the three and a half years of drought. Ahab had not only searched Israel high and low for Elijah, he had literally rattled the cages of all of the other nations around them trying to find him, seeing if he had hidden out there!

How very interesting; the man who wanted nothing to do with God's man during the good times of sin was suddenly very interested in finding him once the cost of that sin started coming due.

DO seek out God and God's man before you ever start to go down the road of sin; it is a much better option than trying to find them once everything in your world has fallen apart!

Personal Notes:

Devotion 42

Elijah told Obadiah to go tell Ahab that he was there. Obadiah expressed his concern that if he did and the Spirit of God carried Elijah away somewhere, Obadiah himself would be killed. But Elijah assured Obadiah that he would be right there waiting and would that very day speak to Ahab face to face.

So, Obadiah went and found the king and brought him to where Elijah was. And when Ahab and Elijah met face to face for the first time in more than three years, a very telling exchange took place.

1 Kings 18:17 *And it came to pass, when Ahab saw Elijah, that Ahab said unto him, Art thou he that troubleth Israel?* **18** *And he answered, I have not troubled Israel; but thou, and thy father's house, in that ye have forsaken the commandments of the LORD, and thou hast followed Baalim.*

Ahab accused Elijah of being the one causing all of the trouble in Israel. Lots of times, when Christians get hit with things like that, they respond "meekly and timidly." Elijah did not do so. He threw it right back in Ahab's face and said in so many words, "If you want to know who the problem is around here, look at your latest family portrait. You did this. You. Your sin is the reason all of this is happening."

The world expects Christians to be soft, quiet, timid. God expects something very different of us. While never being coarse or profane, DO stand up and tell the truth about sin and what it has caused and is causing!

Personal Notes:

Devotion 43

After throwing Ahab's accusation right back in his face, Elijah started naming names and giving numbers:

1 Kings 18:19 *Now therefore send, and gather to me all Israel unto mount Carmel, and the prophets of Baal four hundred and fifty, and the prophets of the groves four hundred, which eat at Jezebel's table.*

This was the root cause of all of the turmoil and judgment in Israel. God's people, who should have been worshiping Him alone, were being led into idol worship by their very own king and queen. Ahab, for his part, was following Baal and had four hundred and fifty "prophets for profit" on his payroll. Jezebel, naturally, had taken things even one step farther. While she only had four hundred so called prophets on her payroll, her "prophets of the grove," worshipers of Venus, sometimes called Asherah, actually ate at her table. She had made them part of the royal household.

And it is the very fact that they ate at her table that so intrigues me. You see, while the nation was starving to death, the people who were causing all of the trouble were being well nourished and, therefore, saw no need to change a thing. This type of arrangement even today is why so many people never see the need to repent and forsake their sin!

As hard as it is to see people we love do without, DO be willing to do so if it is their sin that has caused the problem. A "well-fed sinner" will likely always be a sinner!

Personal Notes:

Devotion 44

With Ahab and Jezebel on the throne, and with eight hundred fifty well-fed false prophets leading people into the worship of Baal and Asherah, it would seem logical to assume that the people had totally forsaken the worship of Jehovah God. But in reality, they had done something far worse than that.

1 Kings 18:20 *So Ahab sent unto all the children of Israel, and gathered the prophets together unto mount Carmel.* **21** *And Elijah came unto all the people, and said, How long halt ye between two opinions? if the LORD be God, follow him: but if Baal, then follow him. And the people answered him not a word.*

Rather than forsaking God, which would have been horrible enough all by itself, the people instead just lumped Him in with Baal and Asherah, and "followed all of them." This, above all things, is abhorrent to God. Throughout the Scripture, mixing the holy with the unholy has always brought the strongest condemnation and judgment. Knowing this, Elijah said something that sounds shocking to us: "If Baal is God, then serve him, but if Jehovah is God, then serve Him."

Simply put, the real God, whoever He is, is worth more than a "fence-straddling believer"; He is worth every ounce of our devotion and discipleship.

DO get off the fence. Go all out, all for God, all the time!

Personal Notes:

_____
_____
_____
_____
_____
_____
_____
_____
_____
_____
_____
_____
_____
_____
_____
_____
_____
_____
_____
_____
_____
_____
_____
_____
_____
_____

Devotion 45

The gauntlet had been thrown down, and the prophets of Baal would be first up to bat. All the people were watching to see which "god" would answer by fire. With the pressure on and unable to utilize their standard trick of hot coals and dry tinder under the altar, the prophets of Baal went all out trying to get Baal to answer by fire.

1 Kings 18:26 *And they took the bullock which was given them, and they dressed it, and called on the name of Baal from morning even until noon, saying, O Baal, hear us. But there was no voice, nor any that answered. And they leaped upon the altar which was made.*

What a spectacle! For several hours, these prophets for profit cried out to Baal, leaped up and down on the altar, and got absolutely no response. There was plenty of activity, plenty of "worship," but no reality behind any of it. And when Elijah finally spoke, notice the tender, tolerant, respectful manner in which he did so:

1 Kings 18:27 *And it came to pass at noon, that Elijah mocked them, and said, Cry aloud: for he is a god; either he is talking, or he is pursuing, or he is in a journey, or peradventure he sleepeth, and must be awaked.*

He mocked them! He actually made fun of them out loud in front of everybody! Can you just imagine if there had been a social media "Christian mob" in that day: "Typical fundamentalist, making fun of other religions! #Eyeroll #Coexist #Tolerance."

And yet Elijah was exactly right to do what he did. The prophets of Baal were leading people to hell, destroying a nation, and bringing "pretend fire" up until they were called out on it.

To everything there is a season, and sometimes the correct season is "Mocktober." In the face of absolute ridiculousness, DO be willing to give that foolishness just exactly as much "respect" as it actually deserves!

Personal Notes:

_____

_____

_____

_____

_____

_____

_____

_____

_____

_____

_____

_____

_____

_____

_____

_____

_____

_____

_____

_____

_____

_____

Devotion 46

Elijah mocked, but the prophets of Baal would not be dissuaded quite yet in their efforts. It took the entire day for their foolishness to fizzle out.

1 Kings 18:28 *And they cried aloud, and cut themselves after their manner with knives and lancets, till the blood gushed out upon them.* **29** *And it came to pass, when midday was past, and they prophesied until the time of the offering of the evening sacrifice, that there was neither voice, nor any to answer, nor any that regarded.*

It is at this point that one almost begins to feel sorry for these foolish followers of a fake god. They went at it all day long. They cut themselves with knives until blood gushed out all over them. And yet at no point did any of them seem to stop and ask themselves the most obvious question: "What kind of a god would expect this of us and then not even answer when we call out to him?"

And yet that scene is replayed with great regularity, especially in Latin America, where many Catholics beat themselves with whips and even have themselves crucified for several hours. Self-flagellation is also practiced among many Shia Muslims on the Day of Ashura, with men slashing their chests with knives and beating their own backs with chains.

And yet, all of it is unnecessary, simply because "Jesus paid it all, all to Him I owe, sin had left a crimson stain, He washed it white as snow!"

DO remember that Jesus paid it all. God does not expect you to bleed for Him to earn His favor; He bled for you so that you could be given His grace!

Personal Notes:

_____
_____
_____
_____
_____
_____
_____
_____
_____
_____
_____
_____
_____
_____
_____
_____
_____
_____
_____
_____
_____
_____
_____
_____
_____
_____
_____
_____

Devotion 47

After letting the prophets of Baal have an entire day to cry out to the heedless god fashioned by their own hands, Elijah took his turn at the plate. After an entire day of failure by the prophets of Baal and with everyone watching to see if Elijah could do any better, how would he start? What would he do first? To Elijah, that was an easy question to answer.

1 Kings 18:30 *And Elijah said unto all the people, Come near unto me. And all the people came near unto him. And he repaired the altar of the LORD that was broken down.*

Calling all the people close to him, Elijah turned and looked at the altar of God which was laying in ruins, and he rebuilt it. If there would ever be a revival in the land, if there would ever be a restoration to God's favor, he knew that it had to start right there. The altar of God, the place where God's people prayed, offered sacrifice, and communed with God, had to be set up and utilized once again.

That still holds true to this day. How many family altars are "in ruins" while the garish lights of the brand-new television are in pristine condition and flashing brightly all day every day? How many church altars have given way to entertainment stages? How many vehicle seats used to be the site of long hours praying to the God of heaven as we drove and now are just comfortable spots to listen to talk radio?

Ouch. Do you want a revival in your own life? It will have to begin by rebuilding the altar. So DO rebuild the altar!

Personal Notes:

_____
_____
_____
_____
_____
_____
_____
_____
_____
_____
_____
_____
_____
_____
_____
_____
_____
_____
_____
_____
_____
_____
_____
_____
_____
_____
_____

Devotion 48

Elijah had repaired the altar of God on the top of Mount Carmel. This would have been a very old altar, dating either from the time before all worship was directed to Jerusalem or from some time after the division of the kingdom when true worshipers longed for the ability to get to Jerusalem and yet could not do so because of Jeroboam and every wicked king that succeeded him.

This altar, long since ruined, was repaired and would now be taken one step further by Elijah.

1 Kings 18:31 *And Elijah took twelve stones, according to the number of the tribes of the sons of Jacob, unto whom the word of the LORD came, saying, Israel shall be thy name:* **32** *And with the stones he built an altar in the name of the LORD: and he made a trench about the altar, as great as would contain two measures of seed.*

With the wood of the old altar in place, Elijah added twelve stones and a trench to it. The twelve stones were a reminder that God never intended for the kingdom to be divided; it was their own disobedience that had caused that judgement. But something of an even more practical nature should be observed concerning this altar, namely the fact that there was another perfectly good, very much available altar already there! The altar that the prophets of Baal had been using all day long was still in perfect shape, since their "god" had not sent fire down onto it. Why not just use that one? Why go to all the hours and effort to remake and enhance Jehovah's altar instead? The answer is because that is exactly what their problem was at that very moment, mixing their devotion between Baal and Jehovah, halting between two opinions rather than being "either/or" on the subject.

DO understand that, no matter what it takes, God expects our worship of Him to be undiluted, never mixed with anything different or impure!

Personal Notes:

_____

_____

_____

_____

_____

_____

_____

_____

_____

_____

_____

_____

_____

_____

_____

_____

_____

_____

_____

_____

_____

_____

_____

_____

Devotion 49

The trench about Elijah's rebuilt altar was about to serve a most remarkable purpose.

1 Kings 18:33 *And he put the wood in order, and cut the bullock in pieces, and laid him on the wood, and said, Fill four barrels with water, and pour it on the burnt sacrifice, and on the wood.* **34** *And he said, Do it the second time. And they did it the second time. And he said, Do it the third time. And they did it the third time.* **35** *And the water ran round about the altar; and he filled the trench also with water.*

Mount Carmel overlooked the sea, so even in the drought this water was easy enough to come by. Twelve barrels of it were procured and then poured out onto the sacrifice and the altar, utterly drenching everything. The trenches around the altar completely filled up with water. For years the prophets of Baal had utilized trickery to get the people to "believe." Elijah was not going to do that. If Jehovah was really God, He would not need help from dry tinder, hidden coals, and dancing prophets with flowing robes, and Elijah knew it. He just wanted to make sure that everyone else knew it as well.

I wish that the concept of using trickery to get people to believe was just a thing of the past. But I have heard way too many people using trickery, sales techniques, and outright lies to get people to say a prayer for me to believe that trickery amongst even Christians does not exist today.

Do you believe in God? Then DO be honest when you evangelize or preach or witness. God does not need your sleight of hand, and it is an insult to Him to imagine otherwise!

Personal Notes:

Devotion 50

The stage was set. The drama had been building all day long as the prophets of Baal danced and screamed and cried out to their false god. Exhausted and unsuccessful, they retired from the contest as Elijah took his turn. Elijah repaired the altar, dug a trench around it, drenched everything with water, and then stepped forward to pray. And after years of God being pushed aside, now that Elijah had reopened the door for Him, He was going to step through that door in an unmistakable way.

1 Kings 18:36 *And it came to pass at the time of the offering of the evening sacrifice, that Elijah the prophet came near, and said, LORD God of Abraham, Isaac, and of Israel, let it be known this day that thou art God in Israel, and that I am thy servant, and that I have done all these things at thy word.* **37** *Hear me, O LORD, hear me, that this people may know that thou art the LORD God, and that thou hast turned their heart back again.* **38** *Then the fire of the LORD fell, and consumed the burnt sacrifice, and the wood, and the stones, and the dust, and licked up the water that was in the trench.*

This fire of God fell from heaven so very powerfully that, like a blast furnace, it consumed the altar, the sacrifice, the water, and even the stones. It was utterly remarkable. Nothing quite like that had ever happened. But as remarkable as that "big" thing is, a very small thing that is actually a huge thing is really what God was after. And He got it.

1 Kings 18:39 *And when all the people saw it, they fell on their faces: and they said, The LORD, he is the God; the LORD, he is the God.*

The. He is THE God. That tiny three letter definite article is what all of this was really about. He is not just a god among others... He is the God, the only God.

DO meditate on that tiny word "the" today. It really does make all the difference!

Personal Notes:

_____
_____
_____
_____
_____
_____
_____
_____
_____
_____
_____
_____
_____
_____
_____
_____
_____
_____
_____
_____
_____
_____
_____
_____

Devotion 51

Everyone now knew who the real God, the only God, was. But the task was still not yet complete.

1 Kings 18:40 *And Elijah said unto them, Take the prophets of Baal; let not one of them escape. And they took them: and Elijah brought them down to the brook Kishon, and slew them there.*

There were four hundred prophets of Baal on the mountain. They were immediately and instantly captured by all of the people surrounding them, people who now knew they had been hoodwinked by these charlatans. But follow this: they were captured on top of the mountain... and then taken down into the valley and killed by the brook Kishon. Isn't that interesting! Why do it that way?

The brook Kishon eventually emptied out into the sea. The blood of these devilish deceivers would not be allowed to stain the soil of God's land; it would be carried away into the depths of the sea and washed from memory.

Aren't you glad that, for the child of God, something else gets carried into the depths of the sea?

Micah 7:19 *He will turn again, he will have compassion upon us; he will subdue our iniquities; and thou wilt cast all their sins into the depths of the sea.*

DO rejoice in the fact that rather than washing your blood and memory away and dropping them into the depths of the sea, God does all of that to your sins instead!

Personal Notes:

Devotion 52

The fire of God had fallen. The people had acknowledged Jehovah as the only God. The prophets of Baal were all dead. But the land was still just as parched, dry, and ruined as ever. But then Elijah gave Ahab some very good news.

1 Kings 18:41 *And Elijah said unto Ahab, Get thee up, eat and drink; for there is a sound of abundance of rain.*

Put your thinking cap on for just a moment. If there was such an abundance of rain that Elijah could hear it, who else should have been able to hear it?

Ahab. But Ahab could not hear it. And the reason he could not hear it is that Elijah was hearing something that he (Elijah) was not actually hearing. Confused yet? Look at what comes next.

1 Kings 18:42 *So Ahab went up to eat and to drink. And Elijah went up to the top of Carmel; and he cast himself down upon the earth, and put his face between his knees,* **43** *And said to his servant, Go up now, look toward the sea. And he went up, and looked, and said, There is nothing...*

The servant could not see a drop of rain falling, because no rain was falling. There was still not even so much as a cloud in the sky. And yet within moments the rain was falling! So I say again, Elijah was hearing something that he was not hearing. We speak of walking by faith; Elijah was hearing by faith! God told him it was going to rain that day, and for Elijah, that was all the "sound of falling rain" that he needed to hear.

DO "hear by faith." If God has said it, let that be the sound that rings through your heart and ears!

Personal Notes:

Devotion 53

Elijah's servant had come back with word that "there was nothing." But nothing very quickly became a whole lot of something!

1 Kings 18:43 *And said to his servant, Go up now, look toward the sea. And he went up, and looked, and said, There is nothing. And he said, Go again seven times.* **44** *And it came to pass at the seventh time, that he said, Behold, there ariseth a little cloud out of the sea, like a man's hand. And he said, Go up, say unto Ahab, Prepare thy chariot, and get thee down, that the rain stop thee not.* **45** *And it came to pass in the mean while, that the heaven was black with clouds and wind, and there was a great rain. And Ahab rode, and went to Jezreel.* **46** *And the hand of the LORD was on Elijah; and he girded up his loins, and ran before Ahab to the entrance of Jezreel.*

The drought had lasted for three and a half years. But what had lasted for three and a half years was entirely erased in a matter of minutes. Our God is that big! But He is also very "small" when He needs to be. Here is what I mean by that. Elijah, God's man, the man who risked everything in all of this, was about to be caught out in an absolute monsoon. But the hand of the Lord came upon him, and he literally outran Ahab's chariot all the way to the city! He was The Flash before there ever was a "The Flash"!

That seems like such a small thing, temporarily giving a man remarkable speed just to get him in out of the rain. But if you are the one out in the rain, it is not such a small thing after all.

DO rejoice in how big our God is but also in how "small" He can be when it is needed!

Personal Notes:

Devotion 54

The fire had fallen and then the rain. Ahab had been a witness to all of it. It seems that that would be more than enough to convince the wicked king to amend his ways. But, sadly, Ahab was not just wicked, he was also weak:

1 Kings 19:1 *And Ahab told Jezebel all that Elijah had done, and withal how he had slain all the prophets with the sword.*

Ahab told Jezebel. Why? Why could he, as both the head of the nation and also (supposedly) the head of his home, not simply just do right?

The need to check with others before you take a stand and do right, whether man, woman, boy, or girl, is always weakness and will always result at some point in doing wrong rather than right. And for Ahab, it would result in him choosing not to follow through on the great revival that the nation was on the verge of experiencing.

DO make up your mind that, you will check with others about lunch choices, vacation choices, maybe even fashion choices (for we clueless men) but never, ever on whether or not to do right. Just DO right!

Personal Notes:

Devotion 55

After Ahab checked in to see what Jezebel thought of what had happened, she answered about how one might expect of a Jezebel.

1 Kings 19:2 *Then Jezebel sent a messenger unto Elijah, saying, So let the gods do to me, and more also, if I make not thy life as the life of one of them by to morrow about this time.*

Jezebel is the perfect picture of everything a woman ought to not want to be. This woman was so much a "Jezebel" that she was still be mentioned by name nearly a thousand years later in the book of the Revelation! This woman stirred up her husband to do wrong, seduced the people into sexual sin, smarted off at authority, and sought to murder the man of God.

In other words, she was pretty much the poster child for modern feminism.

When it comes to a woman, power is not the issue. Any creature that can make a man twice her size babble like an idiot and blush like a school boy, let alone carry another human being in her womb for nine months and then give birth to it is amazingly powerful. The issue is what you dear ladies do with your power. You can either use your power for evil, as Jezebel did, or for good, as sweet spirited examples like Ruth and Mary did.

Ladies, DO refuse to be a Jezebel. And young men, DO have enough sense in that thick skull of yours never to get involved with a Jezebel to begin with!

Personal Notes:

Devotion 56

1 Kings 19:2 *Then Jezebel sent a messenger unto Elijah, saying, So let the gods do to me, and more also, if I make not thy life as the life of one of them by to morrow about this time.* **3** *And when he saw that, he arose, and went for his life, and came to Beersheba, which belongeth to Judah, and left his servant there.*

We now come to one of the most perplexing things in the Bible. Elijah, one of the very greatest prophets of all time, the man who stared down a king and a nation, called fire down from heaven, and destroyed the prophets of Baal, now runs from the threat of a woman.

Matthew Henry said, "Shall we praise him for this? We praise him not. Where was the courage with which he had lately confronted Ahab and all the prophets of Baal? Nay, which kept him by his sacrifice when the fire of God fell upon it? He that stood undaunted in the midst of the terrors both of heaven and earth trembles at the impotent menaces of a proud passionate woman. Lord, what is man! Great faith is not always alike strong. He could not but know that he might be very serviceable to Israel at this juncture, and had all the reason in the world to depend upon God's protection while he was doing God's work; yet he fled."

Elijah had a nation right on the verge of revival and yet pulled back out of fear. But are we really any better? How many times do we have things in marriage or parenting or at work or in some relationship or circumstance right on the verge of going right, and yet, at one last pushback or threat we cut and run, right when we most need to stand?

Starting is good; standing all the way to the end for God, no matter the opposition, is priceless.

DO stand!

Personal Notes:

_____

_____

_____

_____

_____

_____

_____

_____

_____

_____

_____

_____

_____

_____

_____

_____

_____

_____

_____

_____

_____

_____

_____

Devotion 57

1 Kings 19:4 *But he himself went a day's journey into the wilderness, and came and sat down under a juniper tree: and he requested for himself that he might die; and said, It is enough; now, O LORD, take away my life; for I am not better than my fathers.*

From time to time you will hear some well-meaning, yet ill-informed, person make some very wrong yet dogmatic statements about depression. They will tell you that spiritual people do not get depressed and that depression is always a sin and other statements of that nature. But if you should ever find yourself depressed, it may comfort you to know that you are in very good company.

1 Kings 19:4 *But he himself* [Elijah] *went a day's journey into the wilderness, and came and sat down under a juniper tree: and he requested for himself that he might die; and said, It is enough; now, O LORD, take away my life; for I am not better than my fathers.*

Elijah, one of the very greatest prophets in history, so great that he later appeared on the Mount of Transfiguration with Jesus and Moses, was now so depressed that he literally wanted to die. He was utterly hopeless. And he was not the last great person who ever felt that way. Job repeatedly asked to die and cursed the day of his birth. David wrote many Psalms that any knowledgeable person would regard as being written by someone clinically depressed. Even Jesus said, "My soul is exceeding sorrowful, even unto death."

Is there hope and help for depression? Yes, and the next few devotions will deal with that. But for now, DO be helped just by realizing that not only are you not alone, you are actually in the very best of company!

Personal Notes:

_____

_____

_____

_____

_____

_____

_____

_____

_____

_____

_____

_____

_____

_____

_____

_____

_____

_____

_____

_____

_____

_____

_____

_____

_____

_____

_____

_____

Devotion 58

Elijah had been such a powerhouse for God, so very devoted to Him. But when Elijah got weak and depressed, God did not rail on him or cast him away, as some rather hard-nosed clergy seem inclined to do when others get depressed. Look at how God began the process of restoring him.

1 Kings 19:5 *And as he lay and slept under a juniper tree, behold, then an angel touched him, and said unto him, Arise and eat.* **6** *And he looked, and, behold, there was a cake baken on the coals, and a cruse of water at his head. And he did eat and drink, and laid him down again.*

Elijah was exhausted: physically spent and emotionally drained. He had been on the run for three and a half years, he had climbed a mountain, faced down a king, a nation, and hundreds of false prophets. He had physically rebuilt a large altar. He called fire down from heaven. Then in a driving thunderstorm he outran a chariot all the way to Jezreel, ten miles away!

And yet Jezebel sent word that nothing had changed, and she was going to kill him. And so, Elijah ran again, this time more than one hundred miles from Jezreel to Beersheba and then went another day's journey past that out into the wilderness.

And so, God began the process of restoring this depressed man by letting him get some sleep, feeding him a good meal, and then letting him sleep yet again. You see, no one is spiritual enough to "out spiritual" utter exhaustion.

I saw a tweet from a preacher recently that said, "If you sleep three hours less a night you will have forty-five extra days-worth of time a year to serve the Lord." Unless a person is a lazy sloth, I cannot even begin to quantify how stupid that advice is. It is equivalent to writing a prescription guaranteed to cause depression.

Exhaustion is not spiritual, it is dangerous, and it causes depression. DO get enough rest!

Personal Notes:

_____

_____

_____

_____

_____

_____

_____

_____

_____

_____

_____

_____

_____

_____

_____

_____

_____

_____

_____

_____

_____

_____

_____

Devotion 59

Yesterday, we began to examine the solutions to the depression of Elijah, beginning with the need for him to get some rest. Here, then, was the second step in his restoration.

1 Kings 19:5 *And as he lay and slept under a juniper tree, behold, then an angel touched him, and said unto him, Arise and eat.* **6** *And he looked, and, behold, there was a cake baken on the coals, and a cruse of water at his head. And he did eat and drink, and laid him down again.* **7** *And the angel of the LORD came again the second time, and touched him, and said, Arise and eat; because the journey is too great for thee.* **8** *And he arose, and did eat and drink, and went in the strength of that meat forty days and forty nights unto Horeb the mount of God.*

In these verses we find the phrase "arise and eat" twice, "did eat and drink" twice, "cake," "cruse of water," and "meat." Immediately thereafter, the Bible tells us that Elijah *"went in the strength of that meat forty days and forty nights."* It could well be said that Elijah "ate his way out of a depression"! But this food was not "junk food"; it was prepared by an angel of God, and we may therefore safely assume that it was healthy to the body rather than harmful to the body. And the liquid he chased the food down with was not soda or any other sugary drink, it was water.

Americans, more than anyone else, seem to have the habit of eating themselves into a depression. We eat things that are highly processed, loaded with sugar, high in saturated fat, and with very little, if any, nutritional value. Little wonder then that everything from our tight clothing to our overworked heart depresses us!

DO take stock of what and how you eat. Healthy food helps to create healthy bodies which helps to produce healthy attitudes!

Personal Notes:

_____

_____

_____

_____

_____

_____

_____

_____

_____

_____

_____

_____

_____

_____

_____

_____

_____

_____

_____

_____

_____

_____

_____

_____

_____

Devotion 60

We are still dealing with the solutions to the depression of Elijah. We have seen him get some much needed rest and also get some healthy food into his system. But there was still more that went into his rescue from depression.

1 Kings 19:7 *And the angel of the LORD came again the second time, and touched him, and said, Arise and eat; because the journey is too great for thee. 8 And he arose, and did eat and drink, and went in the strength of that meat forty days and forty nights unto Horeb the mount of God.*

When Elijah left Jezreel, he did so on the run for his life. But after he got some rest and food, the angel of God set him moving yet again, this time toward a goal rather than away from a fear. In other words, Elijah got in a good healthy workout! Imagine how good you would feel after taking a forty day walk!

Exercising does a marvelous thing in regard to depression. When a person exercises, their body does exactly what it was designed by God to do. It produces a wonderful set of chemicals known as endorphins. Endorphins reduce pain, produce feelings of happiness and euphoria, help to regulate the appetite, and settle the mind.

A very good friend of mine weighed in at two hundred twenty pounds and was clinically depressed, on anti-depressants, and still nearly suicidal despite the meds. And then he tried something different. He started walking every single day. And then as the weight started coming off, he started running every day. And then as he started to get really lean, he started doing Spartan races. He now weighs about one hundred sixty pounds, isn't on anti-depressants anymore, and is as happy as a lark. For him, his depression was rooted in his poor physical condition and was completely solved by moving his feet.

DO understand that one good way to help deal with depression is to simply put one foot in front of the other for two or three miles once a day!

Personal Notes:

_____
_____
_____
_____
_____
_____
_____
_____
_____
_____
_____
_____
_____
_____
_____
_____
_____
_____
_____
_____
_____
_____
_____

Devotion 61

We have dealt quite a bit with the physical solutions to Elijah's depression, namely rest, good nutrition, and exercise. But there was another type of solution to his depression as well, one that moved beyond the physical.

1 Kings 19:8 *And he arose, and did eat and drink, and went in the strength of that meat forty days and forty nights unto Horeb the mount of God. **9** And he came thither unto a cave, and lodged there; and, behold, the word of the LORD came to him, and he said unto him, What doest thou here, Elijah?*

Elijah took a forty-day journey with a very specific destination in mind, Horeb, the mount of God. You likely know it by its much more famous name, Sinai.

This was the very mountain where God first met with His people and spoke with Moses face to face. Elijah, in his darkest moment of depression, went to where he knew he could meet with God. And that makes him much, much smarter than the average Christian today who in their times of discouragement and depression run the opposite direction.

The house of God is designed for many things, but one of the things God gave it to us for is so that we could meet with Him there in our hardest times. The house of God will always be the most special place on earth to God and the place where He most delights in meeting with His people. So on those days when depression makes you want to stay out, DO make even sure, more than ever, that you actually come and get in!

Personal Notes:

Devotion 62

Elijah had rested, gotten some nutritious food into his system, exercised, gone to meet with God, and begun to actually analyze his problems. But the battle against depression was still yet being fought, and here is the next step God led him to in his recovery.

1 Kings 19:11 *And he said, Go forth, and stand upon the mount before the LORD. And, behold, the LORD passed by, and a great and strong wind rent the mountains, and brake in pieces the rocks before the LORD; but the LORD was not in the wind: and after the wind an earthquake; but the LORD was not in the earthquake:* **12** *And after the earthquake a fire; but the LORD was not in the fire: and after the fire a still small voice.*

Elijah had experienced a lot of noise recently. The showdown on mount Carmel against the prophets of Baal, all of their screaming and devilish dancing. The fire of God falling from heaven powerfully enough to consume the altar, the sacrifice, the rocks, and the water. The sudden violent thunderstorm soaking the land. The rage of Jezebel. His own pounding feet as he ran. And now God would bring the noise again, this time in the form of a wind strong enough to rend the mountains, followed by an earthquake, followed by a fire. Noise, noise, noise, noise!

But then after the fire came a still, small voice. It was as if God was saying, "You have had a lot of noise in your life, my child; it's time for a bit of holy quiet."

We do not know what the voice said. We just know it was still, small, and there was no noise anymore to drown it out.

Is it any wonder that people who are scrolling on their smart phones, while watching 24/7 cable news, while the kids are playing loud video games in the next room, and the dog is barking out back tend to be depressed? Without actual quiet time, how do we ever expect to hear the voice of God in our prayer and Bible reading time, and without hearing the voice of God, how do we ever expect victory over depression?

DO make a habit of having actual, regular QUIET time with the Lord!

Personal Notes:

_____

_____

_____

_____

_____

_____

_____

_____

_____

_____

_____

_____

_____

_____

_____

_____

_____

_____

_____

Devotion 63

The recovery of Elijah was nearing completion. And God, in His wisdom, knew just the next step to take.

1 Kings 19:13 *And it was so, when Elijah heard it, that he wrapped his face in his mantle, and went out, and stood in the entering in of the cave. And, behold, there came a voice unto him, and said, What doest thou here, Elijah?* **14** *And he said, I have been very jealous for the LORD God of hosts: because the children of Israel have forsaken thy covenant, thrown down thine altars, and slain thy prophets with the sword; and I, even I only, am left; and they seek my life, to take it away.* **15** *And the LORD said unto him, Go, return on thy way to the wilderness of Damascus: and when thou comest, anoint Hazael to be king over Syria:* **16** *And Jehu the son of Nimshi shalt thou anoint to be king over Israel: and Elisha the son of Shaphat of Abelmeholah shalt thou anoint to be prophet in thy room.* **17** *And it shall come to pass, that him that escapeth the sword of Hazael shall Jehu slay: and him that escapeth from the sword of Jehu shall Elisha slay.* **18** *Yet I have left me seven thousand in Israel, all the knees which have not bowed unto Baal, and every mouth which hath not kissed him.*

God, once again, asked the exact same question as before, and Elijah answered the same way as before as well. His answer was that he was literally the only one left still serving God. And if that had been true, it would certainly have been a depressing thing! The only problem was, it wasn't true, not even close. And Elijah actually knew it; he had already been told of one hundred other prophets hidden in a cave by Obadiah! But God informed him that it was better than that; there were 7,000 people in Israel who had refused to follow Baal, people who would not so much as even bow the knee before him.

Depression has us making mountains out of molehills. And while molehills are an issue, they are not as serious of an issue as mountains! So DO refuse to ever overstate your problems; accuracy is an antidote to depression!

Personal Notes:

_____

_____

_____

_____

_____

_____

_____

_____

_____

_____

_____

_____

_____

_____

_____

_____

_____

_____

_____

_____

Devotion 64

The rescue of Elijah from his desperate depression was almost complete, there was just one more step to be taken.

1 Kings 19:19 *So he departed thence, and found Elisha the son of Shaphat, who was plowing with twelve yoke of oxen before him, and he with the twelfth: and Elijah passed by him, and cast his mantle upon him.* **20** *And he left the oxen, and ran after Elijah, and said, Let me, I pray thee, kiss my father and my mother, and then I will follow thee. And he said unto him, Go back again: for what have I done to thee?* **21** *And he returned back from him, and took a yoke of oxen, and slew them, and boiled their flesh with the instruments of the oxen, and gave unto the people, and they did eat. Then he arose, and went after Elijah, and ministered unto him.*

This was done by the command of God to Elijah in verse sixteen. Elijah, lonely, depressed Elijah, went and made a friend, and then spent the rest of his life pouring himself into him, teaching Elisha and training him. Yes, Elisha ministered to Elijah, but Elijah took that farm boy and turned him into a mighty prophet of God! Had Elijah not come by his way, Elisha would have lived and died in the obscurity of the farm, and none of us would even know his name.

Depression always turns our focus inward to us and our problems. But turning that focus back outward changes our mood dramatically! It is impossible to serve and help others without brightening your own day along the way.

Whatever darkness you are facing, DO find ways to turn your focus outward and be a blessing and help to others. "I" is a one letter prescription for depression, "others" is a six letter prescription for joy!

Personal Notes:

_____

_____

_____

_____

_____

_____

_____

_____

_____

_____

_____

_____

_____

_____

_____

_____

_____

_____

_____

_____

_____

_____

_____

Devotion 65

Once Elijah left the cave and his depression behind, the scene of Scripture shifted back to the palace and King Ahab. It seems that he had himself a bit of problem:

1 Kings 20:1 *And Benhadad the king of Syria gathered all his host together: and there were thirty and two kings with him, and horses, and chariots: and he went up and besieged Samaria, and warred against it.* **2** *And he sent messengers to Ahab king of Israel into the city, and said unto him, Thus saith Benhadad,* **3** *Thy silver and thy gold is mine; thy wives also and thy children, even the goodliest, are mine.*

When Benhadad, king of Syria, besieged the city, he gave Ahab a list of demands. The main bulk of the demands was as follows, "I am taking all of your wives and children." How would Ahab, as a husband especially, respond to such a thing?

1 Kings 20:4 *And the king of Israel answered and said, My lord, O king, according to thy saying, I am thine, and all that I have.*

Wow! Ahab did not even hesitate to offer to give his wife away! Why in the world would he so quickly agree to that? Maybe because his main wife was, of course, Jezebel.

I suspect that, while feigning sadness on the outside, Ahab was probably dancing like Michael Jackson on the inside!

Ladies, DO be so pleasant and so godly that your husband would rather lay down his life than lose you. And young men, DO marry a girl so pleasant and godly that you would die to keep her rather than, after a few miserable years, be glad to be rid of her!

Personal Notes:

Devotion 66

When Benhadad demanded Ahab's wives and children, Ahab immediately agreed. But then Benhadad came back with a new set of demands:

1 Kings 20:5 *And the messengers came again, and said, Thus speaketh Benhadad, saying, Although I have sent unto thee, saying, Thou shalt deliver me thy silver, and thy gold, and thy wives, and thy children;* **6** *Yet I will send my servants unto thee to morrow about this time, and they shall search thine house, and the houses of thy servants; and it shall be, that whatsoever is pleasant in thine eyes, they shall put it in their hand, and take it away.*

His first demand had been people. His second demand was "stuff." Look how Ahab responded:

1 Kings 20:7 *Then the king of Israel called all the elders of the land, and said, Mark, I pray you, and see how this man seeketh mischief: for he sent unto me for my wives, and for my children, and for my silver, and for my gold; and I denied him not.* **8** *And all the elders and all the people said unto him, Hearken not unto him, nor consent.* **9** *Wherefore he said unto the messengers of Benhadad, Tell my lord the king, All that thou didst send for to thy servant at the first I will do: but this thing I may not do. And the messengers departed, and brought him word again.*

How interesting that Ahab was willing to give up family but balked at losing things! That is a man with his priorities seriously out of order.

Throughout your life you will be faced with choices between people and things. Many people have lost their families by pursuing bigger and better things. DO be wiser than that. God did not breathe the breath of life into things, just into people!

Personal Notes:

_____

_____

_____

_____

_____

_____

_____

_____

_____

_____

_____

_____

_____

_____

_____

_____

_____

_____

_____

_____

_____

_____

_____

_____

_____

_____

_____

_____

Devotion 67

Quick! Think of three words that you would use to describe Ahab...

I would use words like wicked, selfish, and foolish. I imagine your words would likely be much the same. Which makes what we see next such a jaw dropping occurrence:

1 Kings 20:12 *And it came to pass, when Benhadad heard this message, as he was drinking, he and the kings in the pavilions, that he said unto his servants, Set yourselves in array. And they set themselves in array against the city.* **13** *And, behold, there came a prophet unto Ahab king of Israel, saying, Thus saith the LORD, Hast thou seen all this great multitude? behold, I will deliver it into thine hand this day; and thou shalt know that I am the LORD.*

God sent a prophet to Ahab. And the message He sent him with was exactly the opposite of what I would expect! Rather than a "you are getting what you deserve, heathen," kind of message, God sent him a message that He would deliver him from Benhadad!

But it was not for any goodness on Ahab's part. It was, in God's own words, so that Ahab would *"know that I am the LORD."*

So often God does what He does, not because we have been "good boys and girls," but because He in His mercy wants us to know Him.

DO rejoice to know that God is way more merciful than we give Him credit for!

Personal Notes:

Devotion 68

Benhadad, king of Syria, had come against Samaria and King Ahab. God had assured Ahab that he would deliver those enemies from Syria into their hands.

1 Kings 20:14 *And Ahab said, By whom? And he said, Thus saith the LORD, Even by the young men of the princes of the provinces. Then he said, Who shall order the battle? And he answered, Thou.* **15** *Then he numbered the young men of the princes of the provinces, and they were two hundred and thirty two: and after them he numbered all the people, even all the children of Israel, being seven thousand.* **16** *And they went out at noon. But Benhadad was drinking himself drunk in the pavilions, he and the kings, the thirty and two kings that helped him.* **17** *And the young men of the princes of the provinces went out first; and Benhadad sent out, and they told him, saying, There are men come out of Samaria.* **18** *And he said, Whether they be come out for peace, take them alive; or whether they be come out for war, take them alive.*

When Ahab led his forces into battle, Benhadad was, shall we say, "busy at the moment." To put it bluntly, it was the middle of the day, and he was drunk. And all of the other kings who had come out to help him were drunk along with him. That explains why he gave such a foolish command that, whoever was coming out against them, they were to be taken alive. That did not work out, at all:

1 Kings 20:19 *So these young men of the princes of the provinces came out of the city, and the army which followed them.* **20** *And they slew every*

one his man: and the Syrians fled; and Israel pursued
them: and Benhadad the king of Syria escaped on an
horse with the horsemen.

Nothing good ever comes from drunkenness. And no one ever becomes a drunk without putting the bottle to their lips for the first time. DO abstain completely from alcoholic beverages; nothing can turn what should be the easy victories of life into overwhelming defeats any quicker than alcohol!

Personal Notes:

_____

_____

_____

_____

_____

_____

_____

_____

_____

_____

_____

_____

_____

_____

_____

_____

_____

_____

_____

_____

Devotion 69

After their embarrassing and overwhelming defeat at the hands of tiny Israel, Benhadad and his forces got their heads together to try and figure out what went wrong. Here is what they came up with.

1 Kings 20:23 *And the servants of the king of Syria said unto him, Their gods are gods of the hills; therefore they were stronger than we; but let us fight against them in the plain, and surely we shall be stronger than they.* **24** *And do this thing, Take the kings away, every man out of his place, and put captains in their rooms:* **25** *And number thee an army, like the army that thou hast lost, horse for horse, and chariot for chariot: and we will fight against them in the plain, and surely we shall be stronger than they. And he hearkened unto their voice, and did so.*

The servants of Benhadad proposed two solutions. One of them showed a very good understanding of a particular situation, and the other of them showed a very poor understanding of a different situation. They properly realized that the thirty-two kings who had been leading the troops into battle were incompetent jack-a-dandies, and they wisely proposed replacing them with actual military captains. But they improperly assumed that Israel's God (gods, as they put it) only had power in the hills. They, therefore, assumed that by fighting in the plains they could gain the victory.

In other words, they were entirely correct in one thing while at the same time being entirely incorrect in another. Do you know what that makes them? Humans.

DO understand that the only infallible source of wisdom in this world is God and His Word. Every human being is entirely capable of being insightful and brilliant on one thing while being clueless on the very next!

Personal Notes:

_____

_____

_____

_____

_____

_____

_____

_____

_____

_____

_____

_____

_____

_____

_____

_____

_____

_____

_____

_____

_____

_____

_____

_____

Devotion 70

Benhadad and Syria had licked their wounds and regrouped, and round two of the battle was about to begin.

1 Kings 20:26 *And it came to pass at the return of the year, that Benhadad numbered the Syrians, and went up to Aphek, to fight against Israel.* **27** *And the children of Israel were numbered, and were all present, and went against them: and the children of Israel pitched before them like two little flocks of kids; but the Syrians filled the country.* **28** *And there came a man of God, and spake unto the king of Israel, and said, Thus saith the LORD, Because the Syrians have said, The LORD is God of the hills, but he is not God of the valleys, therefore will I deliver all this great multitude into thine hand, and ye shall know that I am the LORD.*

Just to say that this was a mismatch would be an understatement of Biblical proportions. Israel was wildly, hysterically outnumbered and "outgunned." And yet, God promised the victory and delivered:

1 Kings 20:29 *And they pitched one over against the other seven days. And so it was, that in the seventh day the battle was joined: and the children of Israel slew of the Syrians an hundred thousand footmen in one day.* **30** *But the rest fled to Aphek, into the city; and there a wall fell upon twenty and seven thousand of the men that were left. And Benhadad fled, and came into the city, into an inner chamber.*

A nation who had just experienced a revival on Mount Carmel was now being reminded yet again that there is no power on earth capable of standing before the God of heaven. By all human understanding, they should have lost this battle, and yet, they won it solely because of God.

DO remember that America will never be safe simply because of her beautiful flag or powerful military; a nation can only be safe when the Lord is their God!

Personal Notes:

_____

_____

_____

_____

_____

_____

_____

_____

_____

_____

_____

_____

_____

_____

_____

_____

_____

_____

_____

_____

_____

_____

_____

_____

Devotion 71

Proud Benhadad, king of Syria, had been defeated and was hiding in the inner chamber of the city of Aphek. Realizing that all was lost, they decided to beg for mercy.

1 Kings 20:31 *And his servants said unto him, Behold now, we have heard that the kings of the house of Israel are merciful kings: let us, I pray thee, put sackcloth on our loins, and ropes upon our heads, and go out to the king of Israel: peradventure he will save thy life. 32 So they girded sackcloth on their loins, and put ropes on their heads, and came to the king of Israel, and said, Thy servant Benhadad saith, I pray thee, let me live. And he said, Is he yet alive? he is my brother. 33 Now the men did diligently observe whether any thing would come from him, and did hastily catch it: and they said, Thy brother Benhadad. Then he said, Go ye, bring him. Then Benhadad came forth to him; and he caused him to come up into the chariot.*

He is my brother?!? Insert mental picture of hand slapping forehead, please...

Um, excuse me, Ahab, your "brother" said he was going to take your wife and children. Your "brother" threatened to level your entire city to the ground and take everything from everyone. Your "brother" came to war against you. Your "brother" slandered your God. Your "brother" would not have hesitated to kill you if he got the chance. You, sir, are as dumb as an umbrella made of toilet tissue. You are the kind of genius that would drown on the back of a pickup truck if it drove off into the river because you could not get the tailgate down to get out.

There is no person on earth so stupid as the person who regards the wrong kind of people as "brothers" or "sisters" or "BFFs" or "their squad" or pick your current modern descriptive term for people you are close to. It takes an actual fool to get close to people who are going to ruin them. And yet people do it all time, especially young people, but even older people at times as well.

DO have enough functioning brain cells in your head and enough wisdom in those brain cells to never, ever be close to people who are going ruin you or lead you down the path of ruin!

Personal Notes:

_____

_____

_____

_____

_____

_____

_____

_____

_____

_____

_____

_____

_____

_____

_____

_____

_____

_____

_____

Devotion 72

After Ahab let Benhadad go, God commissioned a prophet to confront him over it.

1 Kings 20:38 *So the prophet departed, and waited for the king by the way, and disguised himself with ashes upon his face. 39 And as the king passed by, he cried unto the king: and he said, Thy servant went out into the midst of the battle; and, behold, a man turned aside, and brought a man unto me, and said, Keep this man: if by any means he be missing, then shall thy life be for his life, or else thou shalt pay a talent of silver. 40 And as thy servant was busy here and there, he was gone. And the king of Israel said unto him, So shall thy judgment be; thyself hast decided it. 41 And he hasted, and took the ashes away from his face; and the king of Israel discerned him that he was of the prophets. 42 And he said unto him, Thus saith the LORD, Because thou hast let go out of thy hand a man whom I appointed to utter destruction, therefore thy life shall go for his life, and thy people for his people.*

In vivid picture form, the prophet pointed out the sin of Ahab in allowing Benhadad to live. That sin was so grievous to God that God was going to require the life of Ahab as payment. Benhadad was utterly wicked, and God had appointed Ahab to destroy him.

You see, when it comes to human government, the first commandment God gave was this:

Genesis 9:6 *Whoso sheddeth man's blood, by man shall his blood be shed: for in the image of God made he man.*

Capital punishment is the foundation of God-ordained human government. And for government to allow murderers to go free is not "showing mercy"; it is actually refusing to show mercy on past victims and potential future victims!

DO understand that capital punishment is ordained by God, and there will always be a price to pay when a society produces a government that no longer fulfills this responsibility.

Personal Notes:

_____

_____

_____

_____

_____

_____

_____

_____

_____

_____

_____

_____

_____

_____

_____

_____

_____

_____

_____

_____

Devotion 73

1 Kings 21 brings us to a passage filled with nobility and scoundrels. And it all begins with a simple piece of land.

1 Kings 21:1 *And it came to pass after these things, that Naboth the Jezreelite had a vineyard, which was in Jezreel, hard by the palace of Ahab king of Samaria.* **2** *And Ahab spake unto Naboth, saying, Give me thy vineyard, that I may have it for a garden of herbs, because it is near unto my house: and I will give thee for it a better vineyard than it; or, if it seem good to thee, I will give thee the worth of it in money.* **3** *And Naboth said to Ahab, The LORD forbid it me, that I should give the inheritance of my fathers unto thee.*

In order to understand what happened in these verses, you should know that the Mosaic law, both in Leviticus 25 and Numbers 36, forbid any of the land that God gave to a tribe from being sold away out of that tribe. It was to always "stay in the family." This was God's gift to His people, and He expected them to enjoy it and hand it down, not treat it like a commodity to be turned into profit.

So, what king Ahab asked was wrong, illegal, utterly forbidden, and Naboth knew it. So this hitherto unknown man, facing off against a wicked, dangerous king, bravely and politely "held his ground."

Oh, how desperately that type of spirit is needed among God's people today!

In these days when it seems like people are "selling out" left and right, DO bravely and politely "hold the ground" that God has given you!

Personal Notes:

Devotion 74

Ahab had been rebuffed by Naboth in his attempt to buy ground that Naboth was not allowed to sell. So how would Ahab, a full-grown adult, respond?

1 Kings 21:4 *And Ahab came into his house heavy and displeased because of the word which Naboth the Jezreelite had spoken to him: for he had said, I will not give thee the inheritance of my fathers. And he laid him down upon his bed, and turned away his face, and would eat no bread.*

Laid down upon his bed... turned away his face... would not eat.

No, this is not a three-year-old we are reading about. It is, as I have said, an actual "adult." And yet this adult was in the midst of a whining, pouting, sobbing, self-thrown pity party. Cue the black balloons, make sure all of the music is in a minor key, and grab this guy a blankie and a pacifier; adulting is just too hard for him today.

How pathetic.

Contrary to popular belief, no one gets to always have their way in this life. Sometimes we get told "no." Sometimes we lose, and real life gives no participation trophies. Sometimes we truly do have to "suck it up, buttercup."

Nothing is less attractive than a whiny, pouting adult. So, child of God, DO learn to leave pouting to the infants; real adults have better things to do!

Personal Notes:

_____
_____
_____
_____
_____
_____
_____
_____
_____
_____
_____
_____
_____
_____
_____
_____
_____
_____
_____
_____
_____
_____
_____
_____
_____

Devotion 75

If the story had ended with Ahab simply pouting like a child, that would have been bad enough. But, sadly, it only got worse from there. Enter Jezebel...

1 Kings 21:5 *But Jezebel his wife came to him, and said unto him, Why is thy spirit so sad, that thou eatest no bread?* **6** *And he said unto her, Because I spake unto Naboth the Jezreelite, and said unto him, Give me thy vineyard for money; or else, if it please thee, I will give thee another vineyard for it: and he answered, I will not give thee my vineyard.* **7** *And Jezebel his wife said unto him, Dost thou now govern the kingdom of Israel? arise, and eat bread, and let thine heart be merry: I will give thee the vineyard of Naboth the Jezreelite.*

Jezebel's assumption and assertion in the first half of verse seven is shocking. Her belief is that, since Ahab is "in charge," he can do what he wants and have what he wants. But the last half of the verse is even more dire; she simply says in so many words, "You want the vineyard? Cheer up; I will give it to you."

It did not belong to her.

Yet, she was going to "give" it to someone else.

Or, put another way, Jezebel was an early socialist. Government existed, in her mind, to "redistribute" wealth and material. And those at the top of any government that goes that way will always have their snouts first in line at the trough.

Theft is theft, even when you call it something that sounds much nicer, like socialism. DO recognize it for what it is, and fight against it with all your might!

Personal Notes:

_____

_____

_____

_____

_____

_____

_____

_____

_____

_____

_____

_____

_____

_____

_____

_____

_____

_____

_____

_____

_____

_____

_____

_____

_____

_____

Devotion 76

Once Jezebel promised to steal, er, I mean "give" the property of Naboth to her husband, Ahab, she quickly set her wicked plan into motion.

1 Kings 21:8 *So she wrote letters in Ahab's name, and sealed them with his seal, and sent the letters unto the elders and to the nobles that were in his city, dwelling with Naboth.* **9** *And she wrote in the letters, saying, Proclaim a fast, and set Naboth on high among the people:* **10** *And set two men, sons of Belial, before him, to bear witness against him, saying, Thou didst blaspheme God and the king. And then carry him out, and stone him, that he may die.* **11** *And the men of his city, even the elders and the nobles who were the inhabitants in his city, did as Jezebel had sent unto them, and as it was written in the letters which she had sent unto them.*

So much of this is staggering to consider. The elders of the city held proof positive in their hands that the queen was framing a man and having him murdered, and yet rather than protect the innocent and charge the guilty, the gutless wonders went right along with it. Naboth was charged, falsely accused, framed, and put to death, when every single person involved, all of them, knew it was not true.

But more staggering to consider is the fact that Naboth was probably not at all surprised by any of it. Everyone in the entire land knew what a demon Jezebel was and that to cross her or her sissy husband meant certain death. She had already threatened to kill no less than Elijah himself!

In other words, Naboth stood for right knowing that it would likely cost him everything, including his life. That, friends, is real bravery.

DO stand for what is right. Naboth did so and is still being spoken of as a hero nearly 3,000 years later!

Personal Notes:

_____

_____

_____

_____

_____

_____

_____

_____

_____

_____

_____

_____

_____

_____

_____

_____

_____

_____

_____

_____

_____

_____

_____

_____

Devotion 77

Back in verse eight, when the framing of Naboth had begun, we read this:

1 Kings 21:8 *So she wrote letters in Ahab's name, and sealed them with his seal, and sent the letters unto the elders and to the nobles that were in his city, dwelling with Naboth.*

When Jezebel wrote the letter sealing Naboth's doom, she did not sign it "Love, Jezebel," she signed it, "Love, Ahab." And yet, when the deed was done, we read this:

1 Kings 21:14 *Then they sent to Jezebel, saying, Naboth is stoned, and is dead.*

This is both sad and a bit funny all at the same time. It is sad that Naboth was killed; it is funny that everyone knew without having to ask that Jezebel was the head of her home and that Ahab was just along for the ride in all of this! If Ahab had been an actual man, the actual head of his home, none of this would have happened to begin with. At worst, it would have been nothing more than a pity party, not a murder. Bad things happen when men refuse to be men.

Men, this world needs real men. And by the way, good women deserve a real man! DO step up and be a real man. Or, if that is too hard for you, please turn in your man card by mail to 5555 Hillary Clinton Avenue, Wimpy County, California.

Personal Notes:

Devotion 78

Naboth was dead, and Jezebel had been informed of it. From there, she went back to her expectant husband with the "good news."

1 Kings 21:15 *And it came to pass, when Jezebel heard that Naboth was stoned, and was dead, that Jezebel said to Ahab, Arise, take possession of the vineyard of Naboth the Jezreelite, which he refused to give thee for money: for Naboth is not alive, but dead.* **16** *And it came to pass, when Ahab heard that Naboth was dead, that Ahab rose up to go down to the vineyard of Naboth the Jezreelite, to take possession of it.*

Quick, answer this question either in your head or out loud. With Naboth dead, who did his property now belong to?

I hope you came up with someone other than "Ahab." You see, even with Naboth dead, there was still not one single line in the law that gave Ahab any right to it! If Naboth had family, the land belonged to them. If he had no family at all, it still belonged to his tribe. Under no circumstances could this land rightly belong to Ahab! And yet he simply strode down to it to take it. You see, everyone had "gotten the message." What Ahab wants, Ahab gets...

But God will never, ever be okay with that.

DO understand that if you get what you get by force or by "powerful connections" or by some other unjust means, there is a God in heaven who sees, knows, and always at some point settles every score on behalf of the innocent!

Personal Notes:

Devotion 79

Ahab's pity party was done. His wife, Jezebel, the acting head of his home, had caused Naboth to be killed, and Ahab was now merrily jaunting down to the vineyard to take it. They were at "the top of the food chain" in Israel; there was no human being in authority over them to make them pay the price for what they had done. But there was, and is, a God in heaven for situations just like that...

1 Kings 21:17 *And the word of the LORD came to Elijah the Tishbite, saying,* **18** *Arise, go down to meet Ahab king of Israel, which is in Samaria: behold, he is in the vineyard of Naboth, whither he is gone down to possess it.* **19** *And thou shalt speak unto him, saying, Thus saith the LORD, Hast thou killed, and also taken possession? And thou shalt speak unto him, saying, Thus saith the LORD, In the place where dogs licked the blood of Naboth shall dogs lick thy blood, even thine.*

Elijah, bold, unashamed Elijah, was called upon once more to confront Ahab. Ahab knew well the power this man had with God; memories of the three-and-a-half-year drought were still fresh in his mind. So, when Elijah showed up with a message of judgment, Ahab knew that it was not a matter of "if," it was just a matter of "when." Elijah told him that neither the crown nor his broom-riding wife could stay the hand of God's judgment. Naboth had bled out and died because of him, the dogs had unceremoniously licked up his blood, and Ahab would face the exact same fate in the exact same spot.

DO understand that there is no height of human power to which you can ascend that will place you above the judging hand of God. The good news is, the same thing holds true of everyone else as well!

Personal Notes:

_____

_____

_____

_____

_____

_____

_____

_____

_____

_____

_____

_____

_____

_____

_____

_____

_____

_____

_____

_____

_____

_____

_____

_____

_____

_____

_____

_____

Devotion 80

Ahab had been justly confronted by the man of God for his heinous crime. How would he respond?

1 Kings 21:20 *And Ahab said to Elijah, Hast thou found me, O mine enemy? And he answered, I have found thee: because thou hast sold thyself to work evil in the sight of the LORD.* **21** *Behold, I will bring evil upon thee, and will take away thy posterity, and will cut off from Ahab him that pisseth against the wall, and him that is shut up and left in Israel,* **22** *And will make thine house like the house of Jeroboam the son of Nebat, and like the house of Baasha the son of Ahijah, for the provocation wherewith thou hast provoked me to anger, and made Israel to sin.* **23** *And of Jezebel also spake the LORD, saying, The dogs shall eat Jezebel by the wall of Jezreel.* **24** *Him that dieth of Ahab in the city the dogs shall eat; and him that dieth in the field shall the fowls of the air eat.*

"Hast thou found me, O mine enemy?" Enemy? Who made it that way? If Elijah was an enemy to Ahab, it was only because Ahab was ever the enemy of God! Ahab should have lived in such a way that Elijah was a friend, not an enemy.

Elijah delivered his message of judgment, and it was harsh. All of Ahab's family would die horrible deaths, and their bodies would be consumed by animals and birds. But special mention was made of Jezebel. She would specifically be eaten by dogs. That was as degrading a death as could be imagined by those people in those days.

It seems that being an enemy of God is not such a good idea after all.

DO rejoice, child of God, that through the sacrifice of Jesus Christ on Calvary, we *"have peace with God through our Lord Jesus Christ"*!

Personal Notes:

_____

_____

_____

_____

_____

_____

_____

_____

_____

_____

_____

_____

_____

_____

_____

_____

_____

_____

_____

_____

_____

_____

_____

_____

_____

_____

_____

_____

_____

Devotion 81

Between the message of judgment that Elijah delivered and the response that Ahab showed, there is a grim two verse commentary on the life of Ahab.

1 Kings 21:25 *But there was none like unto Ahab, which did sell himself to work wickedness in the sight of the LORD, whom Jezebel his wife stirred up.* **26** *And he did very abominably in following idols, according to all things as did the Amorites, whom the LORD cast out before the children of Israel.*

There was no one like Ahab... in the very worst way possible. The text tells us that Ahab "sold himself" to work wickedness in the sight of the Lord, and it further adds that Jezebel "stirred him up" to that wickedness. Ahab did not just follow idols, he did so "abominably." He did all of the things that the Amorites had done, which includes child sacrifice, burning them alive to appease his twisted "gods."

Yes, Ahab sold himself to the very devil of hell. And what price exactly can one receive that makes that a worthwhile bargain?

Child of God, the devil wants people to "sell themselves" to do wickedness. But DO remember that Christ our Savior "gave Himself" so that we could be saved and live for Him in righteousness!

Personal Notes:

Devotion 82

God's message of judgment to Ahab had been delivered. And Ahab justly deserved absolutely everything he had coming to him. And that is what makes what we see next so amazing.

1 Kings 21:27 *And it came to pass, when Ahab heard those words, that he rent his clothes, and put sackcloth upon his flesh, and fasted, and lay in sackcloth, and went softly.* **28** *And the word of the LORD came to Elijah the Tishbite, saying,* **29** *Seest thou how Ahab humbleth himself before me? because he humbleth himself before me, I will not bring the evil in his days: but in his son's days will I bring the evil upon his house.*

Ahab was still going to die a horrible death, and the dogs were still going to lick up his blood. The rest of the judgment on his household was coming too, but it would be delayed until after the death of Ahab. Ahab, the worst of the worst of the worst, the measuring stick for evil in Israel, received mercy from God just by humbling himself before Him.

"But wait!" you say, "He didn't deserve any mercy!"

No, he didn't. But if he had deserved it, it wouldn't be mercy to begin with! By definition, mercy is never a "deserved" thing! And if God was willing to show mercy to Ahab, how much more is He willing to show mercy to us who have received His darling Son as our Savior?

When the devil shows you "you," DO turn right around and show him Jesus! Mercy is ours, every single day, because of Him!

Personal Notes:

Devotion 83

A few quiet (relatively speaking) years passed in Israel. And then came a very unfortunate meeting between Ahab, king of Israel, and Jehoshaphat, king of Judah.

1 Kings 22:1 *And they continued three years without war between Syria and Israel.* **2** *And it came to pass in the third year, that Jehoshaphat the king of Judah came down to the king of Israel.* **3** *And the king of Israel said unto his servants, Know ye that Ramoth in Gilead is ours, and we be still, and take it not out of the hand of the king of Syria?* **4** *And he said unto Jehoshaphat, Wilt thou go with me to battle to Ramothgilead? And Jehoshaphat said to the king of Israel, I am as thou art, my people as thy people, my horses as thy horses.*

Somewhere along the line, Ramoth, a city in Gilead that belonged to Israel, had fallen into the hands of Syria. Ahab asked Jehoshaphat to join him in battle to regain it. Jehoshaphat's answer was a "slam your head in a car door" level of stupid:

"I am as thou art, my people as thy people, my horses as thy horses."

This was an unequivocal, unreserved level of commitment. Jehoshaphat, one of the few godly kings Judah ever had, for some reason made the unthinkable mistake of making the most wicked king in history his "BFF"!

Many years later, Amos the prophet would say, *"Can two walk together, except they be agreed?"*

DO determine never to join hearts, hands, and hopes with wicked people. They have no intention of going your way; their only goal is to get you to go theirs!

Personal Notes:

_____

_____

_____

_____

_____

_____

_____

_____

_____

_____

_____

_____

_____

_____

_____

_____

_____

_____

_____

_____

_____

_____

_____

_____

_____

_____

Devotion 84

Having already committed to a league with Ahab, it seems that Jehoshaphat suddenly began to worry a bit. So he asked for a quick "prayer meeting." And that is when things turned funny.

1 Kings 22:5 *And Jehoshaphat said unto the king of Israel, Enquire, I pray thee, at the word of the LORD to day.* **6** *Then the king of Israel gathered the prophets together, about four hundred men, and said unto them, Shall I go against Ramothgilead to battle, or shall I forbear? And they said, Go up; for the Lord shall deliver it into the hand of the king.* **7** *And Jehoshaphat said, Is there not here a prophet of the LORD besides, that we might enquire of him?*

The word "Lord" appears three times in these three verses. But you will notice that twice it is in all capital letters, and once it is not.

Jehoshpahat specifically asked to enquire of the LORD, Jehovah. That put Ahab in a bit of a quandary. He had prophets of Baal, and prophets of the groves, but no actual prophet of Jehovah "on staff." So he went the "quantity over quality" route. He brought in four hundred likely very bewildered "prophets," and they did their thing. Four hundred "preachers" all chanting the exact same pre-packaged message.

I simply cannot imagine why Jehoshaphat was not convinced. To paraphrase, he basically responded, "Um, could we send away the four hundred chanting puppets, please? All I really need is one man who can get ahold of the one true God for me."

172

Quantity will never be a good substitute for quality when it comes to truth. A million liars will never be as good as one truth teller. DO know God and tell the truth, and DO refuse to listen to all of the choreographed liars on the devil's payroll!

Personal Notes:

_____

_____

_____

_____

_____

_____

_____

_____

_____

_____

_____

_____

_____

_____

_____

_____

_____

_____

_____

_____

_____

_____

_____

Devotion 85

Jehoshaphat had listened with apparent dismay to the four hundred parroting prophets of Ahab. Clearly unsatisfied, he asked for a different kind of a "prophet:"

1 Kings 22:7 *And Jehoshaphat said, Is there not here a prophet of the LORD besides, that we might enquire of him?*

Jehoshaphat very specifically wanted to hear from a prophet of Jehovah, so he asked if there was one of those around. The answer he received is both sad and hilarious.

1 Kings 22:8 *And the king of Israel said unto Jehoshaphat, There is yet one man, Micaiah the son of Imlah, by whom we may enquire of the LORD: but I hate him; for he doth not prophesy good concerning me, but evil. And Jehoshaphat said, Let not the king say so.*

Are you getting that? Please allow me to put it in 21st century context and verbiage: "I hate that preacher because he is always saying mean things to me like 'you are doing wrong' and 'that's a sin' and 'you will answer to God for that.' If he would just say nice things about me, like preachers are supposed to do, I would like him!"

That is EXACTLY the view that the present world and even much of what calls itself Christianity holds! But a preacher who will not warn against sin is about as much use as a doctor who will not warn against obesity and a policeman who will not warn against robbing stores.

DO understand what God made His men to do, and DO thank God if you have one who does!

Personal Notes:

Devotion 86

At Jehoshaphat's insistence, Ahab sent for "that other preacher," Micaiah. While they were fetching him, though, Ahab's prophets held a "camp meeting." And my, what vivid preaching was done!

1 Kings 22:10 *And the king of Israel and Jehoshaphat the king of Judah sat each on his throne, having put on their robes, in a void place in the entrance of the gate of Samaria; and all the prophets prophesied before them. **11** And Zedekiah the son of Chenaanah made him horns of iron: and he said, Thus saith the LORD, With these shalt thou push the Syrians, until thou have consumed them. **12** And all the prophets prophesied so, saying, Go up to Ramothgilead, and prosper: for the LORD shall deliver it into the king's hand.*

Zedekiah was the "big dog preacher" at this meeting. His entire message was built on a really cool illustration using iron horns that he had made. It was, though, a "longhorn" message—a point here, a point there, and a whole lot of bull in between.

Zedekiah was dead wrong in everything he preached that day, and yet everyone there was shouting him on. He literally claimed to be speaking for God, when God was nowhere near any of it.

I have been in a few meetings like that.

DO remember that preaching, whether as calm as a mountain stream or as wild as a tornado, is utterly useless apart from the actual Word of God! But if the Word of God is preached, whether wildly or calmly, it is worth your time to listen!

Personal Notes:

Devotion 87

As the corrupt camp meeting continued, so did the hilarity. The messenger got to Micaiah, informed him that he was "next up to preach," and then made a hysterical request of him.

1 Kings 22:13 *And the messenger that was gone to call Micaiah spake unto him, saying, Behold now, the words of the prophets declare good unto the king with one mouth: let thy word, I pray thee, be like the word of one of them, and speak that which is good.*

Once again today, please allow me to restate this in 21st century context and verbiage. "Micaiah, this has been a good meeting thus far. I mean, REALLY good. It is 'out of the banks'! Please, I am begging you, do not preach anything that will kill the meeting!"

And if the meeting had actually been full of Bible, sound doctrine, and the Holy Spirit, that would have been a very reasonable request.

But it had not been like that at all. And therefore, what was really needed was for someone to have enough God and guts to stride to the pulpit and pour the cold water of truth on all of the devilish fire.

It is hard to imagine, sometimes, but the truth is that not everything going under the guise of religion is right; not all of it is even trying to be right. The devil is not anti-religion; he is actually a religion mogul! The vast majority of what calls itself "of God" in this world is anything but.

DO cast a Biblically based skeptical eye toward religion. Some of it is true, much of it is false, and that which is true will withstand the scrutiny!

Personal Notes:

Devotion 88

Micaiah had been asked to go along with the message of everyone else. And when he got up to preach, his words were the same as everyone else. But as you will see, something in his tone of voice or mannerism was very different!

1 Kings 22:15 *So he came to the king. And the king said unto him, Micaiah, shall we go against Ramothgilead to battle, or shall we forbear? And he answered him, Go, and prosper: for the LORD shall deliver it into the hand of the king.* **16** *And the king said unto him, How many times shall I adjure thee that thou tell me nothing but that which is true in the name of the LORD?*

Had Micaiah even pretended to be sincere, Ahab would have celebrated his message, but Micaiah clearly spoke with such obvious, dripping sarcasm in his voice that Ahab errupted in a fit of anger and demanded the truth.

In other words, he played right into Micaiah's hands. Did he want the truth? He was about to get it whether he wanted it or not:

1 Kings 22:17 *And he said, I saw all Israel scattered upon the hills, as sheep that have not a shepherd: and the LORD said, These have no master: let them return every man to his house in peace.*

The message meant "Ahab, when you go out to this battle, the Lord will not be with you, and you are going to be killed."

That was exactly the message he needed to hear. It also clearly lined up with the warning that Elijah the prophet gave him just one chapter earlier.

Two different men of God gave the same warning in different words.

Ahab would die that day, but it was not God's fault. God sent him the warning, and he ignored it repeatedly.

DO refuse to ever blame God for anything that goes wrong in your life as a result of your own sin. He has given you an entire Bible full of warnings to keep you out of that sin!

Personal Notes:

_____

_____

_____

_____

_____

_____

_____

_____

_____

_____

_____

_____

_____

_____

_____

_____

_____

_____

_____

_____

_____

_____

Devotion 89

As Micaiah continued his message of warning, he gave some of the oddest, most shocking words in the entire Bible.

1 Kings 22:19 *And he said, Hear thou therefore the word of the LORD: I saw the LORD sitting on his throne, and all the host of heaven standing by him on his right hand and on his left.* **20** *And the LORD said, Who shall persuade Ahab, that he may go up and fall at Ramothgilead? And one said on this manner, and another said on that manner.* **21** *And there came forth a spirit, and stood before the LORD, and said, I will persuade him.* **22** *And the LORD said unto him, Wherewith? And he said, I will go forth, and I will be a lying spirit in the mouth of all his prophets. And he said, Thou shalt persuade him, and prevail also: go forth, and do so.* **23** *Now therefore, behold, the LORD hath put a lying spirit in the mouth of all these thy prophets, and the LORD hath spoken evil concerning thee.*

We know from Job 1-2 that all heavenly beings, fallen and unfallen, often are required to come before the Lord and report. On this particular day, God asked all of them, "*Who shall persuade Ahab, that he may go up and fall at Ramothgilead?*" An evil spirit offered to go be a lying spirit in the mouths of all of his false prophets and lead him to his death. And God allowed it.

There is so much we could say about all of that. But for now, just let me say, DO know that when you are of no more use to the devil, he will not hesitate to throw you away like a piece of garbage. He has no love for you; he just wants to use you while he can.

Personal Notes:

Devotion 90

The corrupt camp meeting was just about over. But there was still one more small part to it; a preacher fight. Micaiah had accurately stated that the other prophets there were "filled with the devil." The big-dog preacher of the meeting, Zedekiah, did not take too kindly to that characterization:

1 Kings 22:24 *But Zedekiah the son of Chenaanah went near, and smote Micaiah on the cheek, and said, Which way went the Spirit of the LORD from me to speak unto thee?*

Can you imagine being in a meeting where one preacher punches another one? It would certainly be memorable! But Micaiah, for his part, did not lash back out. He just delivered the word of the true God one more time, this time directly to his assailant.

1 Kings 22:25 *And Micaiah said, Behold, thou shalt see in that day, when thou shalt go into an inner chamber to hide thyself.*

Zedekiah had been brash and vocal during his "preaching," but when the judgment of God fell he would be whimpering and hiding.

Everyone is brave when they are running wild in sin; when the judgment of God finally falls, not so much.

DO have enough sense to realize that if you brazenly run with the devil's crowd now, you will end up sheepishly hiding and trembling in fear later!

Personal Notes:

Devotion 91

Micaiah the prophet gave a crystal-clear prophecy, and it was one hundred eighty degrees different from the prophecy of the false prophets on Ahab's payroll. In other words, both could not possibly be right. According to Micaiah, Ahab was not going to live through the battle. Here was Ahab's indignant response.

1 Kings 22:26 *And the king of Israel said, Take Micaiah, and carry him back unto Amon the governor of the city, and to Joash the king's son;* **27** *And say, Thus saith the king, Put this fellow in the prison, and feed him with bread of affliction and with water of affliction, until I come in peace.*

Ahab commanded that Micaiah be imprisoned and only given the worst possible water and food, and very little of it, until he returned from the battle that Micaiah said he would not survive. This was cruel and arrogant, but to Micaiah, it was not the biggest issue. The biggest issue was whether he was actually, provably, the prophet of God. So here is how he responded.

1 Kings 22:28 *And Micaiah said, If thou return at all in peace, the LORD hath not spoken by me. And he said, Hearken, O people, every one of you.*

Micaiah knew, and was willing to tell everyone, that the mark of a true prophet of God was unfailing, one hundred percent accuracy in every "prophetic utterance." Miss even once, even a little, and it meant you were not, in fact, a true prophet.

Remember that here and now in our modern 21st century, and DO hold so called prophets to that same Biblical standard which has never changed.

Many these days love to claim that they are prophets, speaking for God, when they are about as consistent and accurate as a government financial projection!

Personal Notes:

_____

_____

_____

_____

_____

_____

_____

_____

_____

_____

_____

_____

_____

_____

_____

_____

_____

_____

_____

_____

_____

_____

_____

_____

Devotion 92

There is average dumb, and then there is "slam your head repeatedly in a car door" level dumb. I am amazed at how often in Scripture otherwise righteous people devolved into that far low level of stupidity. The following verses show such an example.

1 Kings 22:29 *So the king of Israel and Jehoshaphat the king of Judah went up to Ramothgilead.* **30** *And the king of Israel said unto Jehoshaphat, I will disguise myself, and enter into the battle; but put thou on thy robes. And the king of Israel disguised himself, and went into the battle.*

Do you understand what just happened? King Ahab basically told King Jehoshaphat, "Hey, we're getting ready to go into a heated battle. The enemy will be looking to kill us since we are the two kings. What say I dress as just a normal soldier so as to not draw attention to myself, and you put on all of your shiny finery and draw all the attention to yourself?" To which Jehoshaphat inexplicably said, "Duuuhh, Yup! Sounds like a great idea!"

Jehoshaphat was the godly one of the two and yet was showing all of the wisdom and intelligence of an underdeveloped turnip.

Repeat after me: "Stupidity is not the same thing as godliness; stupidity is not the same thing as godliness; stupidity is not the same thing as godliness."

The world is watching Christians, oh so carefully. They hope to see us as illiterate and illogical. And if they do, they will have all the reason they think they need to reject Christ.

DO be both godly and wise!

Personal Notes:

_____

_____

_____

_____

_____

_____

_____

_____

_____

_____

_____

_____

_____

_____

_____

_____

_____

_____

_____

_____

_____

_____

_____

_____

_____

_____

_____

Devotion 93

The battle was joined, and the Syrians entered into it under a very specific set of commands.

1 Kings 22:31 *But the king of Syria commanded his thirty and two captains that had rule over his chariots, saying, Fight neither with small nor great, save only with the king of Israel.* **32** *And it came to pass, when the captains of the chariots saw Jehoshaphat, that they said, Surely it is the king of Israel. And they turned aside to fight against him: and Jehoshaphat cried out.*

There was one very specific person the king of Syria wanted dead: Ahab. And this was not just a matter of "cut the head off of the snake and the body dies." You see, there was a second large force aligned against Syria that day, Judah, lead by King Jehoshaphat. And yet there was no attempt to target him. In fact, when he cried out and they realized he was the one they were inadvertently pursuing, they simply turned away and let him go!

The king of Syria, by the way, was Benhadad, the very same Benhadad that Ahab had defeated in battle, and rather than put him to death, brought him up into his own chariot and called him "my brother." He let Benhadad go that day. Benhadad broke all of the promises he made, and now Ahab was going to pay the price with his own life.

Never, ever imagine that the wicked have any real loyalty to you. When you cover for them, team up with them, become part of their "squad," all you are doing is laying the foundation for your own destruction.

DO be smarter than that!

Personal Notes:

Devotion 94

When the Syrians realized they were pursuing the wrong king, and that Ahab was therefore somewhere in the battle, disguised and unrecognizable, a most amazing thing happened.

1 Kings 22:33 *And it came to pass, when the captains of the chariots perceived that it was not the king of Israel, that they turned back from pursuing him.* **34** *And a certain man drew a bow at a venture, and smote the king of Israel between the joints of the harness: wherefore he said unto the driver of his chariot, Turn thine hand, and carry me out of the host; for I am wounded.*

There were three sizeable kingdoms involved in this battle. The numbers of soldiers on the field of battle would have been enormous.

Two separate prophets had prophesied the death of Ahab in this battle and place. And yet Ahab had "written himself an insurance policy" against that happening. He disguised himself, knowing that the Syrians were not interested in killing any random soldier. He believed that his disguise was enough to thwart God and render His prophets wrong.

And yet some unnamed, random Syrian soldier, drew his bow *"at a venture,"* meaning "randomly," and shot one random enemy soldier in the midst of the thousands on the battle field, and his arrow randomly ripped squarely into a small random opening in Ahab's armor.

In other words, random only to man, but very specific to God. Ahab lived like the devil, disguised himself to try and stay safe from God's judgment, and found out too late that God is never fooled by disguises, and His arrows never miss.

DO live righteously. That way you never have to try and disguise yourself to begin with to parents, pastor, friends, social media followers, or especially God!

Personal Notes:

_____

_____

_____

_____

_____

_____

_____

_____

_____

_____

_____

_____

_____

_____

_____

_____

_____

_____

_____

_____

_____

_____

_____

_____

_____

_____

Devotion 95

Ahab's life blood was dripping away. But something very specific was about to happen to it.

1 Kings 22:35 *And the battle increased that day: and the king was stayed up in his chariot against the Syrians, and died at even: and the blood ran out of the wound into the midst of the chariot.* **36** *And there went a proclamation throughout the host about the going down of the sun, saying, Every man to his city, and every man to his own country.* **37** *So the king died, and was brought to Samaria; and they buried the king in Samaria.* **38** *And one washed the chariot in the pool of Samaria; and the dogs licked up his blood; and they washed his armour; according unto the word of the LORD which he spake.*

Dogs licked up the blood of Ahab. And, interestingly, they did so in a very, very specific spot:

1 Kings 21:19 *And thou shalt speak unto him, saying, Thus saith the LORD, Hast thou killed, and also taken possession? And thou shalt speak unto him, saying, Thus saith the LORD, In the place where dogs licked the blood of Naboth shall dogs lick thy blood, even thine.*

Innocent Naboth, powerless Naboth, was stoned to death, dogs licked up his blood, and Ahab was responsible. Years later the king himself had dogs lick his own blood from his own dead body in that exact same spot. What are the odds on that?

Impossible, except for one thing: God.

One thing you should always remember about God is that He is very exact. He is precise. So DO trust His Word. For good or bad, when He says it, it is guaranteed!

Personal Notes:

Devotion 96

Ahab was dead. But the Bible gives us a quick, unusual postlude to his life.

1 Kings 22:39 *Now the rest of the acts of Ahab, and all that he did, and the ivory house which he made, and all the cities that he built, are they not written in the book of the chronicles of the kings of Israel?*

Ahab, during his lifetime, built an "*ivory house*," a house adorned with and mostly decorated with ivory. It was a lavish luxury that Amos the prophet railed against. So Ahab, who allowed a man to be killed over a small piece of property, took time during his life to build an elaborate, ivory house for himself.

We speak often of people living in "ivory towers"; Ahab literally did. While others were suffering, he was living large. And not content with just that disparity, he gladly took what little bit others had as well.

I cannot think of a worse testimony or example. By contrast, Jesus, our King, stepped off of His throne, left the palaces of heaven, and came to where we were. He left the street of gold to walk on streets of dirt. He gave up glory for insults, and worship for abuse. What a contrast between two kings!

And yet all of these thousands of years later, the king who built himself an ivory house is still reviled, and the King who became flesh is still revered.

DO understand that an ivory tower life may make you comfortable for a while, but a life lived for others makes you Christ-like!

Personal Notes:

_____

_____

_____

_____

_____

_____

_____

_____

_____

_____

_____

_____

_____

_____

_____

_____

_____

_____

_____

_____

_____

_____

_____

_____

_____

_____

_____

Devotion 97

After the Bible records the death of Ahab, the spotlight shifts fully to Jehoshaphat, king of Judah, for a few verses. And in what we read of him we find both righteousness and a riddle.

1 Kings 22:41 *And Jehoshaphat the son of Asa began to reign over Judah in the fourth year of Ahab king of Israel. 42 Jehoshaphat was thirty and five years old when he began to reign; and he reigned twenty and five years in Jerusalem. And his mother's name was Azubah the daughter of Shilhi. 43 And he walked in all the ways of Asa his father; he turned not aside from it, doing that which was right in the eyes of the LORD: nevertheless the high places were not taken away; for the people offered and burnt incense yet in the high places.*

The righteousness is easy to see in these verses; it is plainly spelled out. The riddle is found when we compare the end of verse forty-three with another verse about him from another book:

2 Chronicles 17:6 *And his [Jehoshaphat's] heart was lifted up in the ways of the LORD: moreover he took away the high places and groves out of Judah.*

One verse tells us he took away the high places, the other verse tells us that he did not. So how is this riddle to be solved? Here is what you need to know. There were two different kinds of "high places" in the Old Testament. One was where idols were worshiped, and the other was where God was worshiped. Once God placed His name and stamp of approval on the temple, there were to be no more high places, no more places where people offered sacrifice.

God spelled that out for them in Deuteronomy 12:1-11. He wanted His people to come to a specific place of His choosing and assemble together to worship and sacrifice.

Assembling together in God's appointed place has always mattered to God. So, DO be faithful to church!

Personal Notes:

_____

_____

_____

_____

_____

_____

_____

_____

_____

_____

_____

_____

_____

_____

_____

_____

_____

_____

_____

_____

_____

_____

_____

_____

_____

Devotion 98

When Ahab died, the Scriptural postlude of his life was that he built a house of ivory. By contrast, look at the very unique Scriptural postlude of the life of King Jehoshaphat:

1 Kings 22:45 *Now the rest of the acts of Jehoshaphat, and his might that he shewed, and how he warred, are they not written in the book of the chronicles of the kings of Judah?* **46** *And the remnant of the sodomites, which remained in the days of his father Asa, he took out of the land.*

Ahab's epitaph dealt with material things; Jehoshaphat's epitaph dealt primarily with moral things. Jehoshaphat clearly understood how God felt about Sodomy and Sodomites, and he removed them from the land. This sin is always condemned in the strongest terms in Scripture; God has never placed His stamp of approval on it, and He never will.

That is not a very popular thing to say in our day. But God leaves "popularity contests" to junior high schools and their close contemporaries, Hollywood awards shows. What God is concerned about is holiness, not tiaras and tin statues.

DO remember that God loved us enough to tell us the truth about sin, and then He died to pay for it!

Personal Notes:

_____

_____

_____

_____

_____

_____

_____

_____

_____

_____

_____

_____

_____

_____

_____

_____

_____

_____

_____

_____

_____

_____

_____

_____

_____

_____

_____

_____

_____

Devotion 99

After recording the end of Jehoshaphat, the Bible then gives us a quick rundown of the life of Ahaziah, king of Israel, son of Ahab and Jezebel. And, as you might expect, it was not good.

1 Kings 22:51 *Ahaziah the son of Ahab began to reign over Israel in Samaria the seventeenth year of Jehoshaphat king of Judah, and reigned two years over Israel.* **52** *And he did evil in the sight of the LORD, and walked in the way of his father, and in the way of his mother, and in the way of Jeroboam the son of Nebat, who made Israel to sin:* **53** *For he served Baal, and worshipped him, and provoked to anger the LORD God of Israel, according to all that his father had done.*

In some cases, seeing a boy follow in daddy's footsteps or seeing a daughter revere her mother is a very good thing. But in this particular case, reading that Ahaziah did "according to all that his father had done" is a horrible, heart-breaking thing.

Sometimes a person simply must break the cycle set by family, even by generations of family.

Some of you had good, godly parents and can safely follow in their footsteps. Others of you, to put it mildly, did not. You who did not need to know that "honoring" your mother and father does not mean "walking in their footsteps."

DO be willing to walk a far different path than anyone who has come before you, if any of those "anyones" were walking the wrong path!

Personal Notes:

Other Books by Dr. Bo Wagner

Beyond the Colored Coat
Daniel: Breathtaking
Don't Muzzle the Ox
Esther: Five Feast and the Finger Prints of God
From Footers to Finish Nails
I'm Saved! Now What???
James: The Pen and the Plumb Line
Jonah: A Study in Greatness
Learning Not to Fear the Old Testament
Marriage Makers/Marriage Breakers
Nehemiah: A Labor of Love
Romans: Salvation From A-Z
Ruth: Diamonds in the Darkness

Fiction Titles

The Night Heroes Series:
Cry From the Coal Mine (Vol. 1)
Free Fall (Vol. 2)
Broken Brotherhood (Vol. 3)
The Blade of Black Crow (Vol. 4)
Ghost Ship (Vol. 5)
When Serpents Rise (Vol. 6)
Moth Man (Vol. 7)
Runaway (Vol. 8)
Terror by Day (Vol. 9)

Sci-Fi

Zak Blue and the Great Space Chase:
Falcon Wing (Vol. 1)